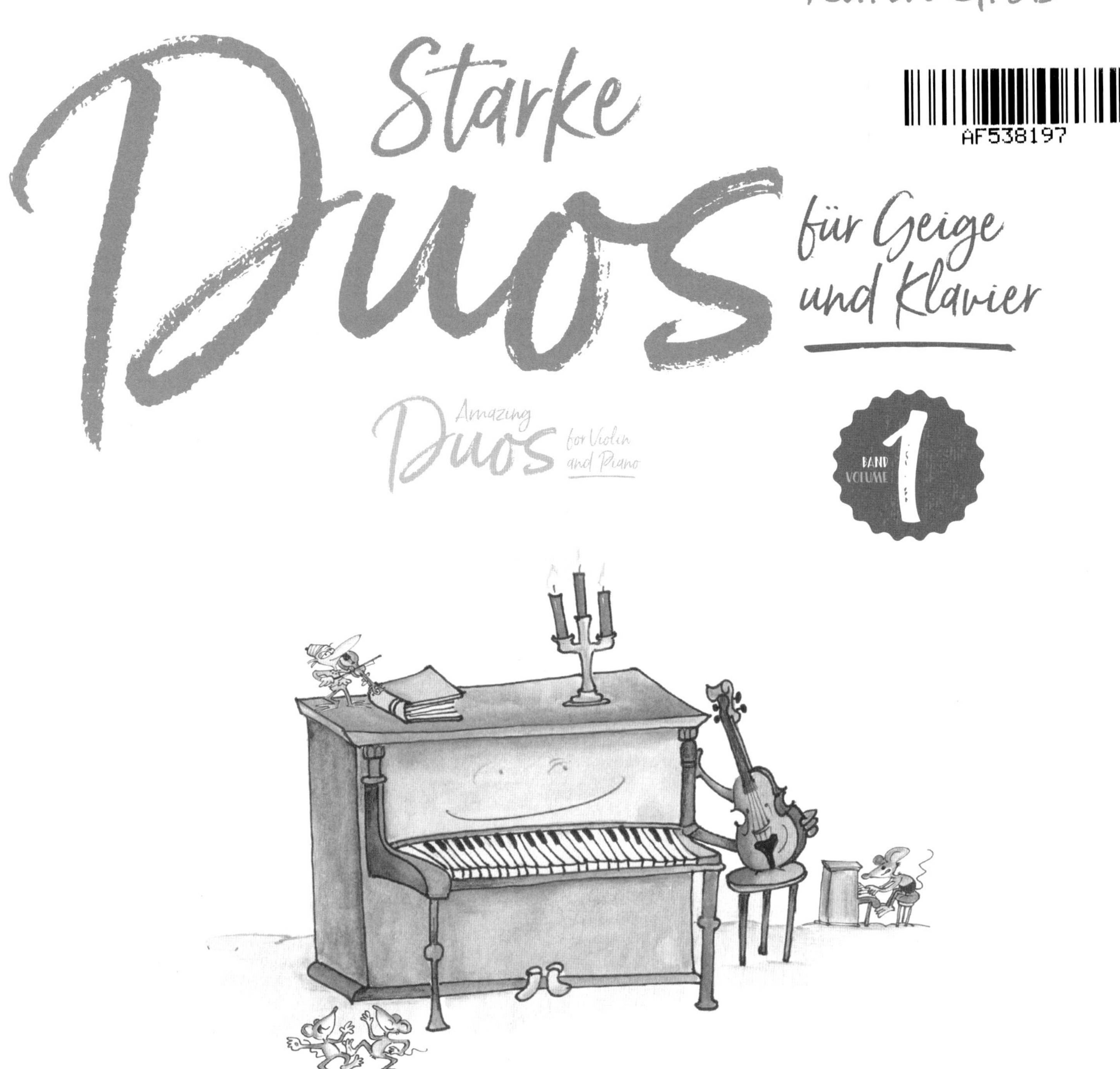

23 Charakterstücke – Leicht in beiden Instrumenten

23 Character Pieces – easy for both instruments

Illustrationen /Illustrations: Wolfgang Steinmeyer

VORWORT

Die leicht erfassbaren Charakterstücke dieser Sammlung wecken Spielfreude. Sie erzählen von Rittern und Seeräubern, malen Landschaftsbilder, lassen Drachen steigen und Frösche quaken oder reisen ins Land der Pandabären …

Mein Ziel war es, ansprechende Stücke zu schreiben, die in beiden Instrumenten ähnlich leicht spielbar sind, so dass sie von Kindern im gleichen Alter musiziert werden können.

Im Mittelpunkt steht das Zusammenspiel: aufeinander hören, im Hintergrund bleiben oder in den Vordergrund treten. Beide Instrumente haben sowohl solistische als auch begleitende Aufgaben. Die Geigenstimme bewegt sich innerhalb der 1. und 2. Griffart. Alle Stücke sind mit Fingersätzen bzw. Strichvorschlägen versehen.

Mein ganz herzlicher Dank gilt Annette Demond (Cello) und Bernd-Udo Winker (Geige und Bratsche) für ihre fachliche Beratung in Streicherfragen!

Karin Groß, Dortmund 2018

PREFACE

The easily accessible character pieces in this collection will be a joy for young musicians to play. They tell of knights and pirates, paint landscapes, have kites flying and frogs croaking or take you to the land of the pandas …

It was my aim to write enchanting pieces which are similarly easy for both instruments so that they can be played by children of the same age.

The focus is on playing together: listening to each other, staying in the background or coming to the fore. Both instruments take solo as well as accompanying roles. The violin part moves within finger patterns one and two. Fingerings and suggestions for bowings are included for all the pieces.

I am extremely grateful to Annette Demond (cello) and Bernd-Udo Winker (violin and viola) for the expert advice they gave me concerning their instruments.

Karin Groß, Dortmund 2018

Impressum

VHR 3435 / ISMN 979-0-2013-1001-5 / ISBN 978-3-86434-101-4

Notensatz: Karin Groß, Dortmund

Illustrationen: Wolfgang Steinmeyer, Waltenhofen
Umschlaggestaltung: Gerhard Illig Kommunikation, Erlangen
Foto: Peter Leßmann, Münster

www.holzschuh-verlag.de

INHALT CONTENTS

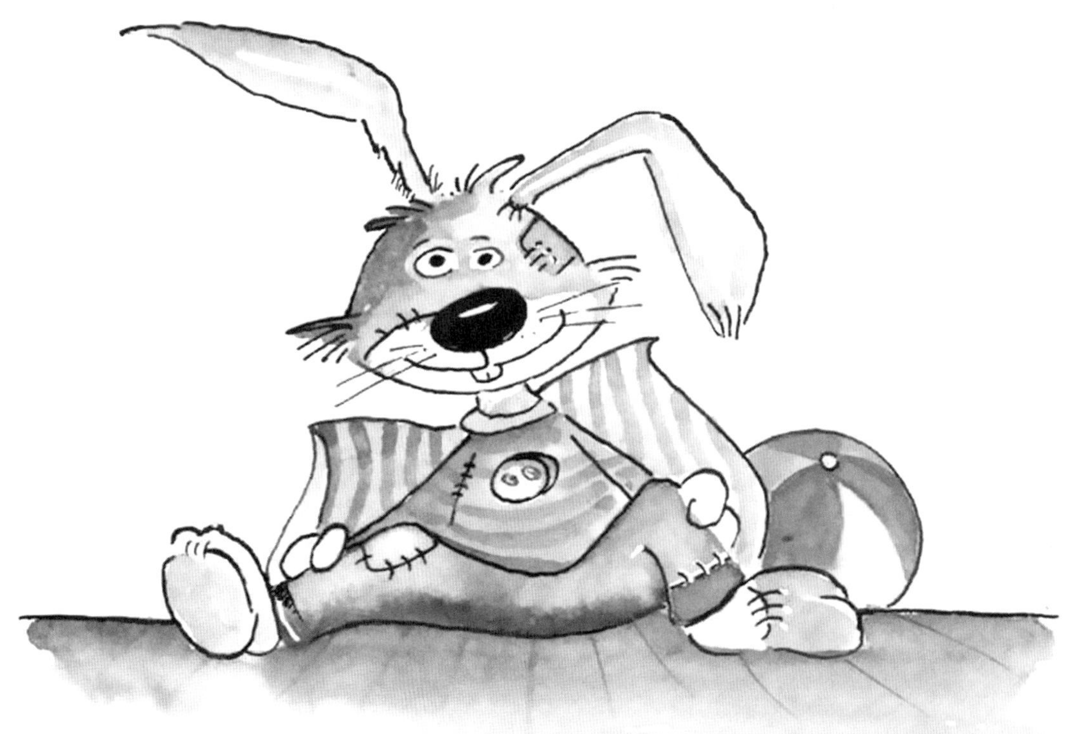

Das Kuscheltier

The Cuddly Toy

Karin Groß

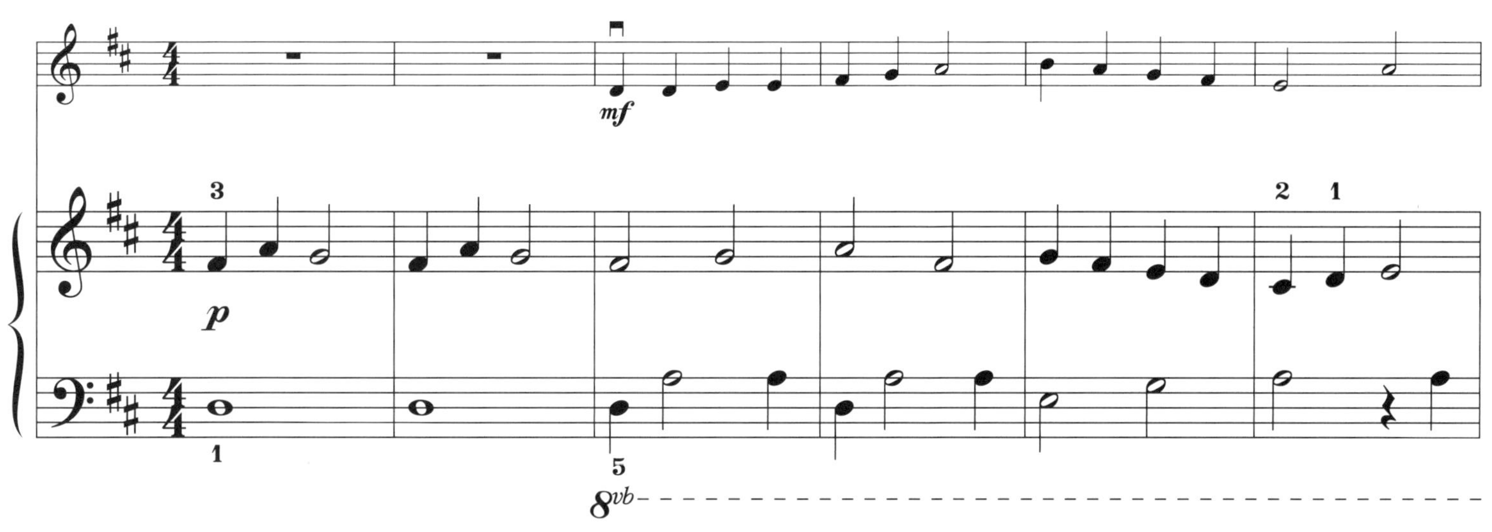

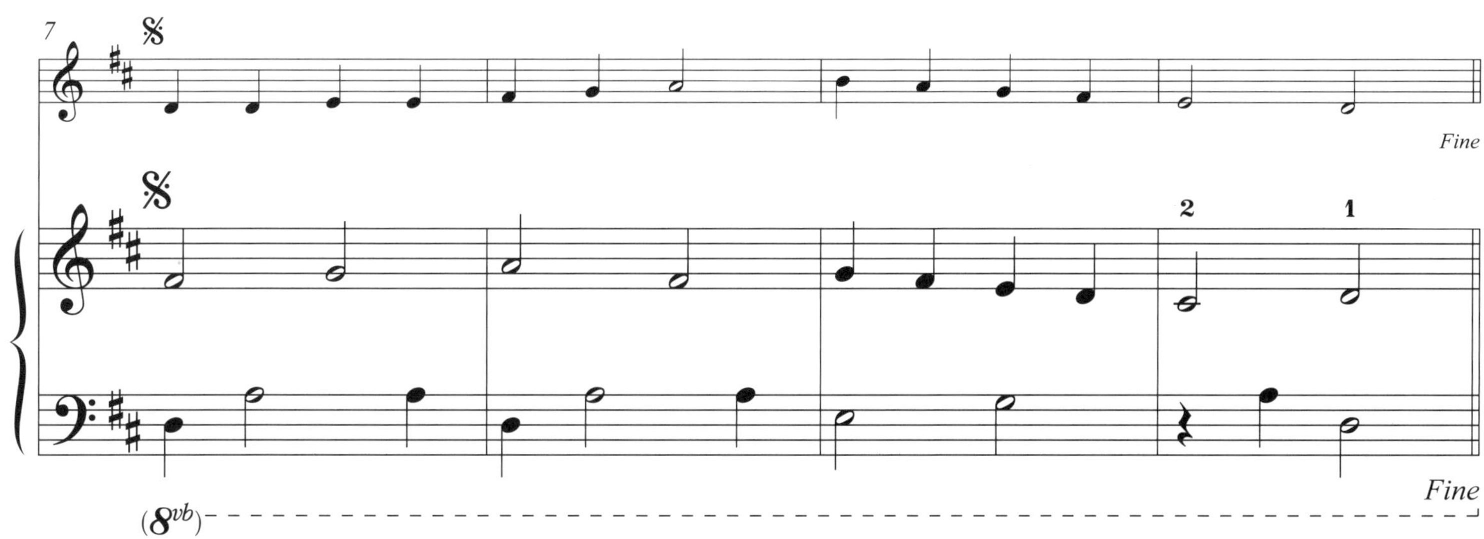

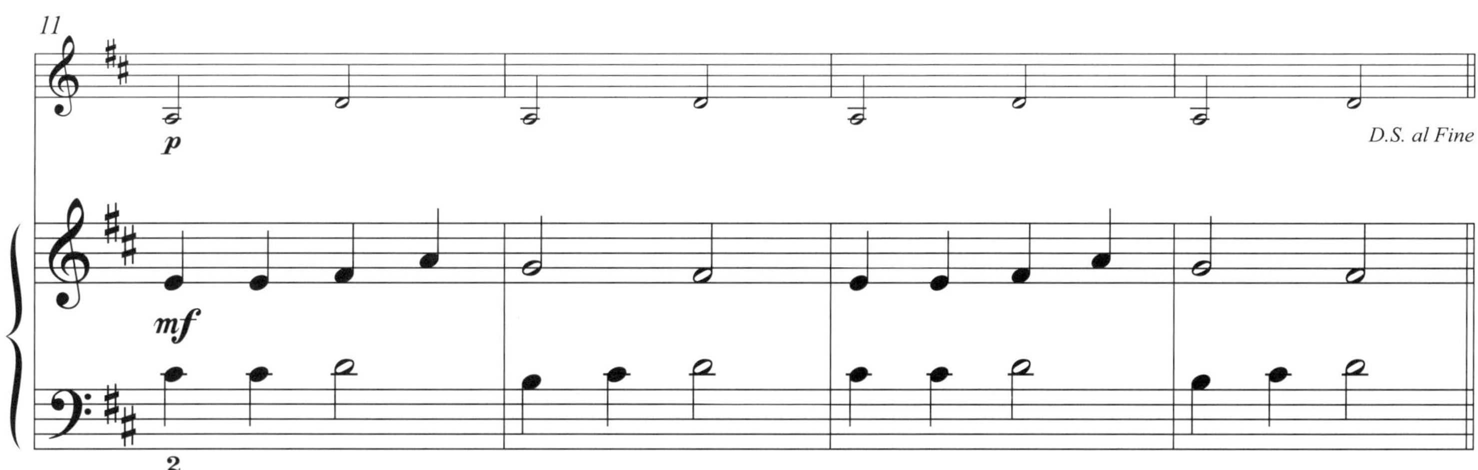

D.S. al Fine

Entenkanon

Duck Canon

Karin Groß

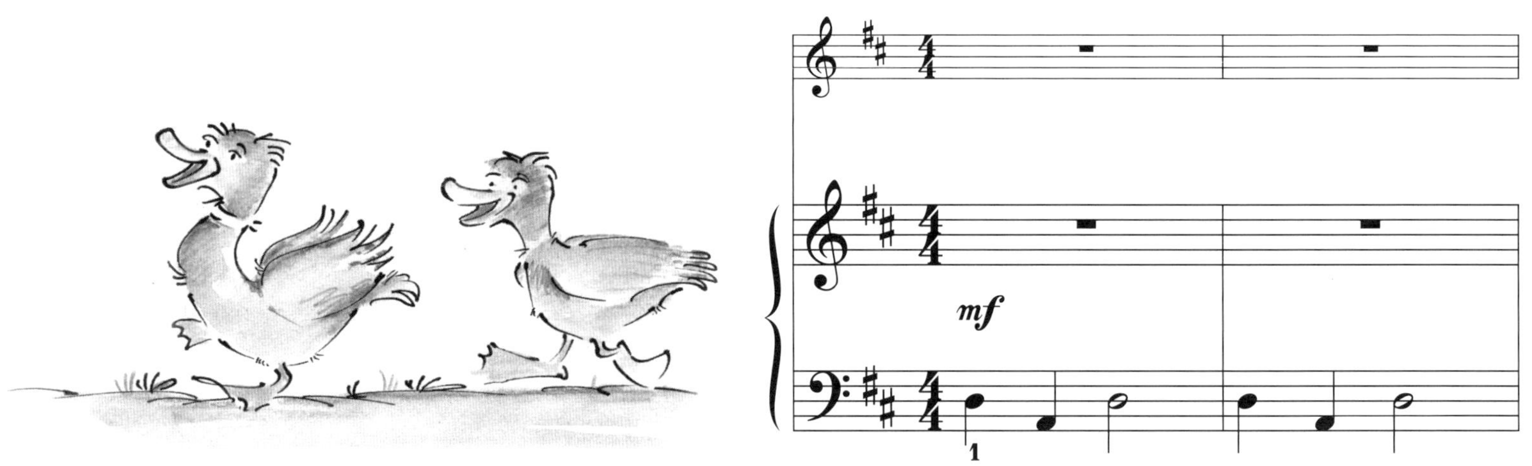

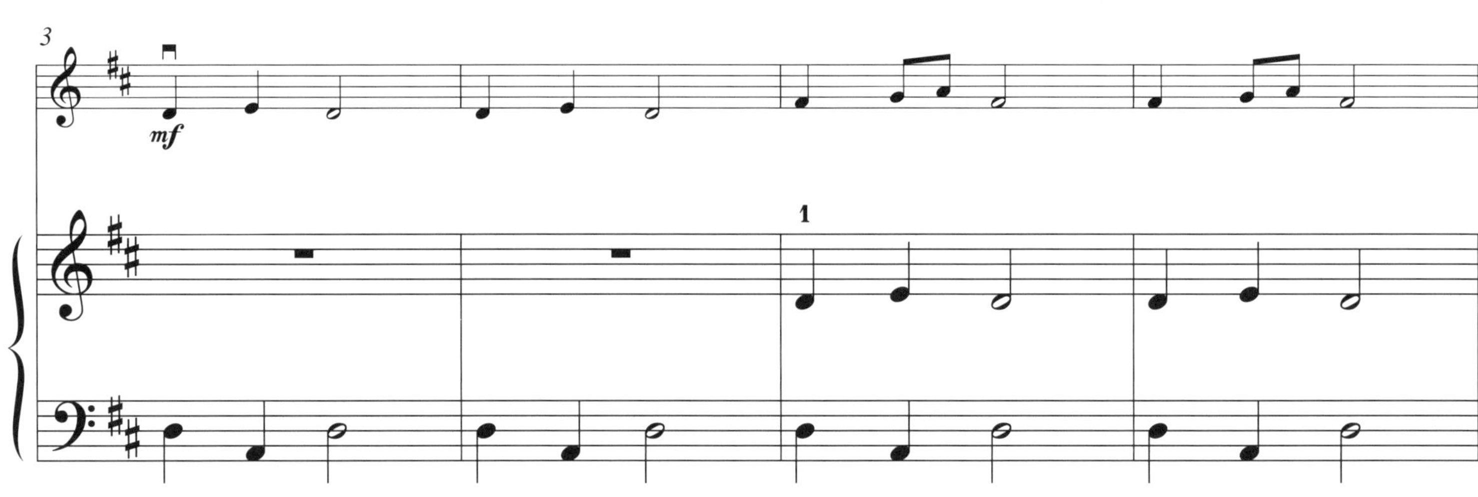

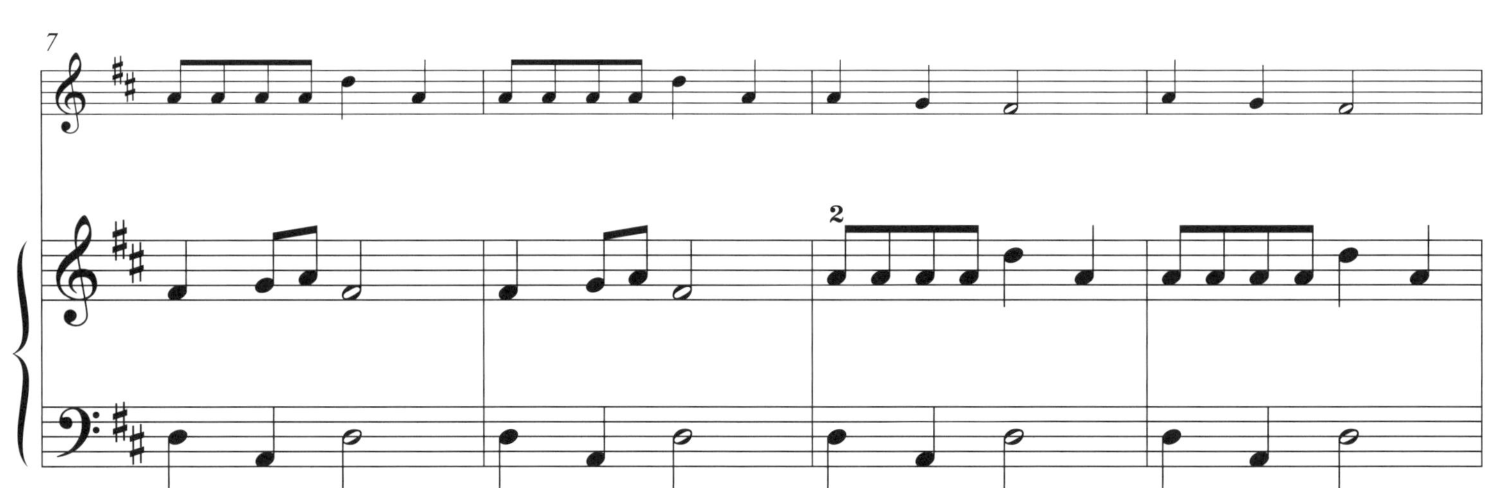

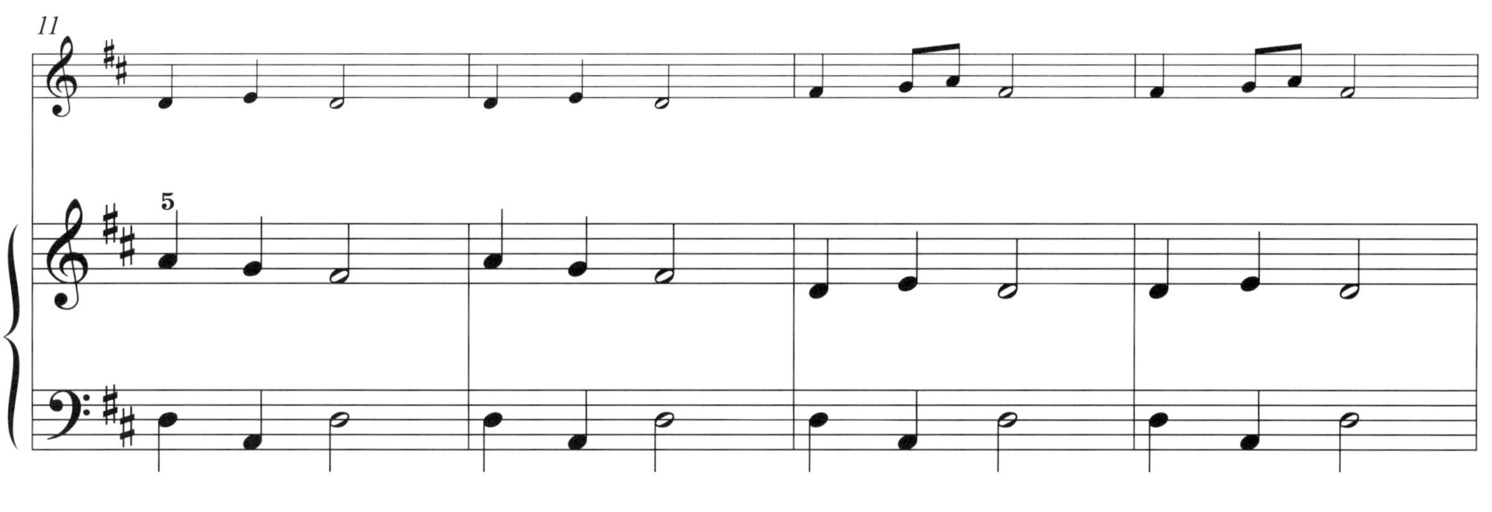
11
5

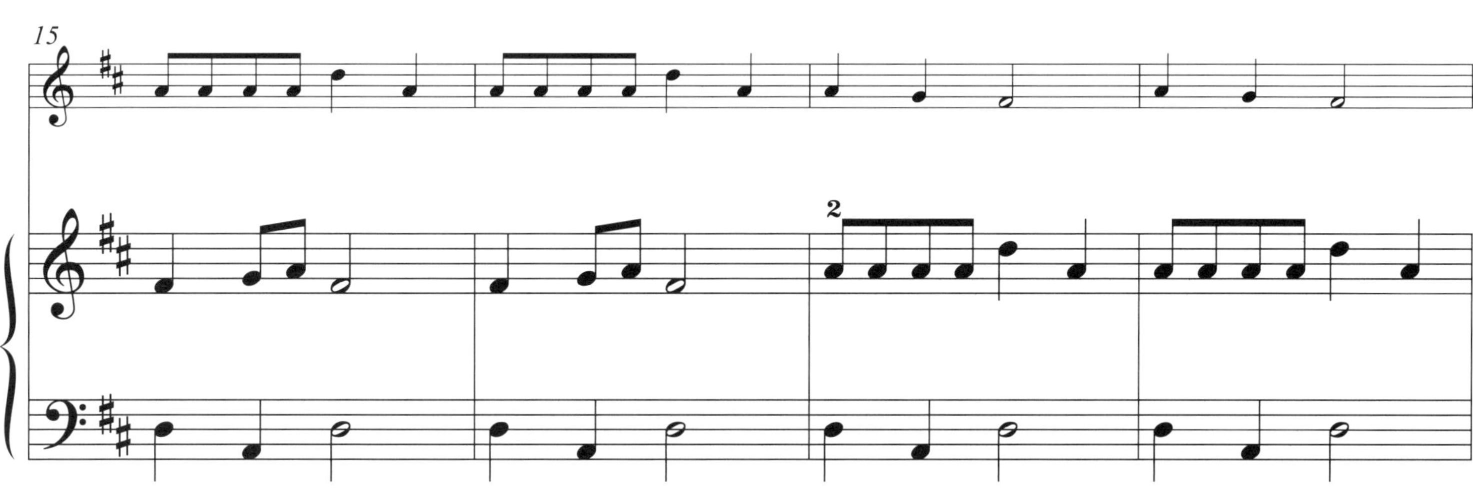
15
2

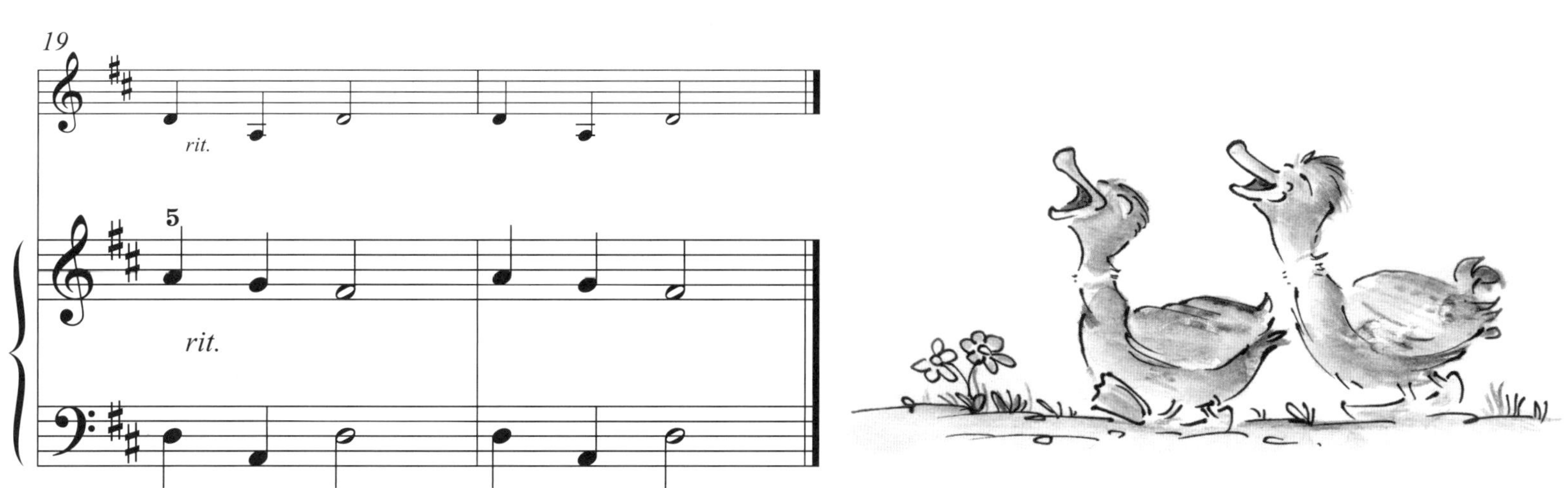
19
rit.
5
rit.

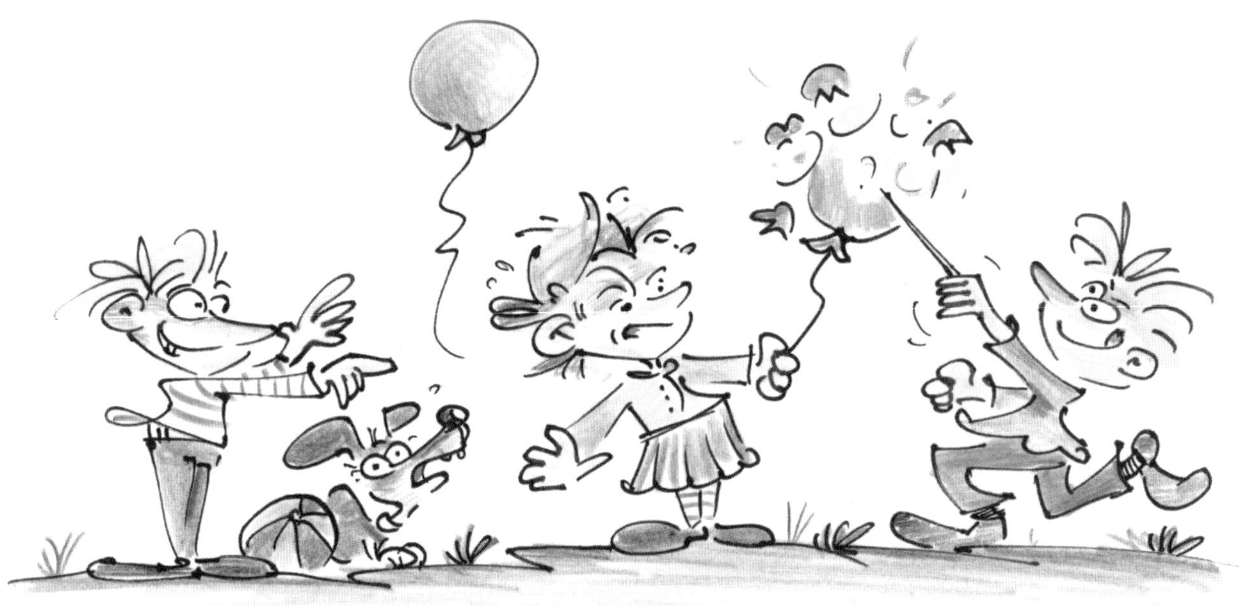

Der gemeine Kerl

A Mean Guy

Karin Groß

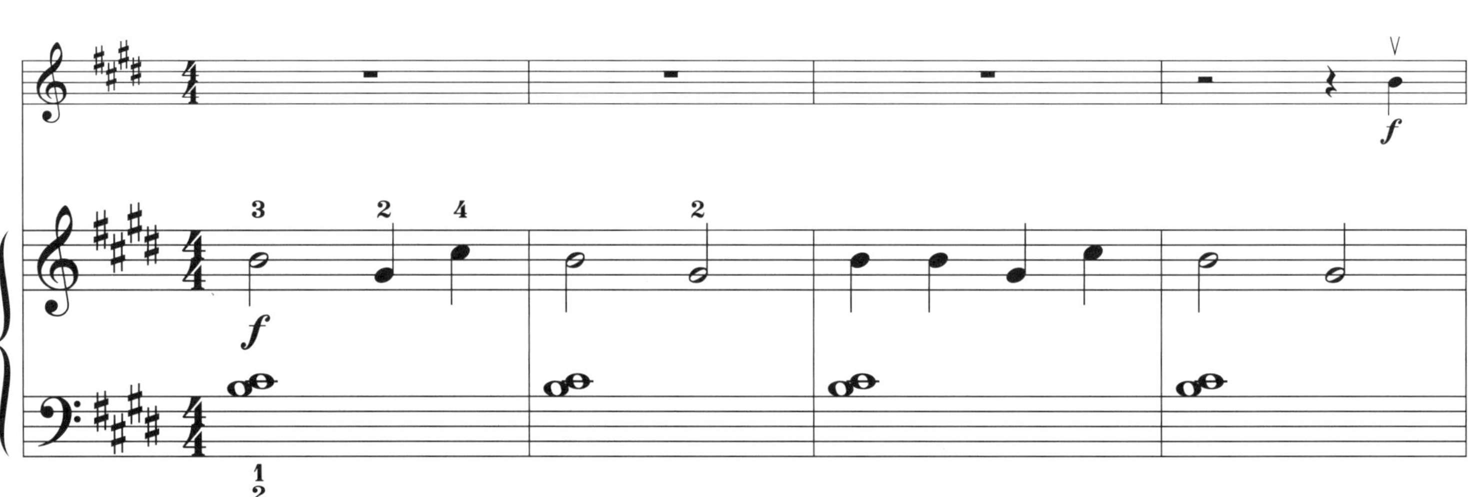

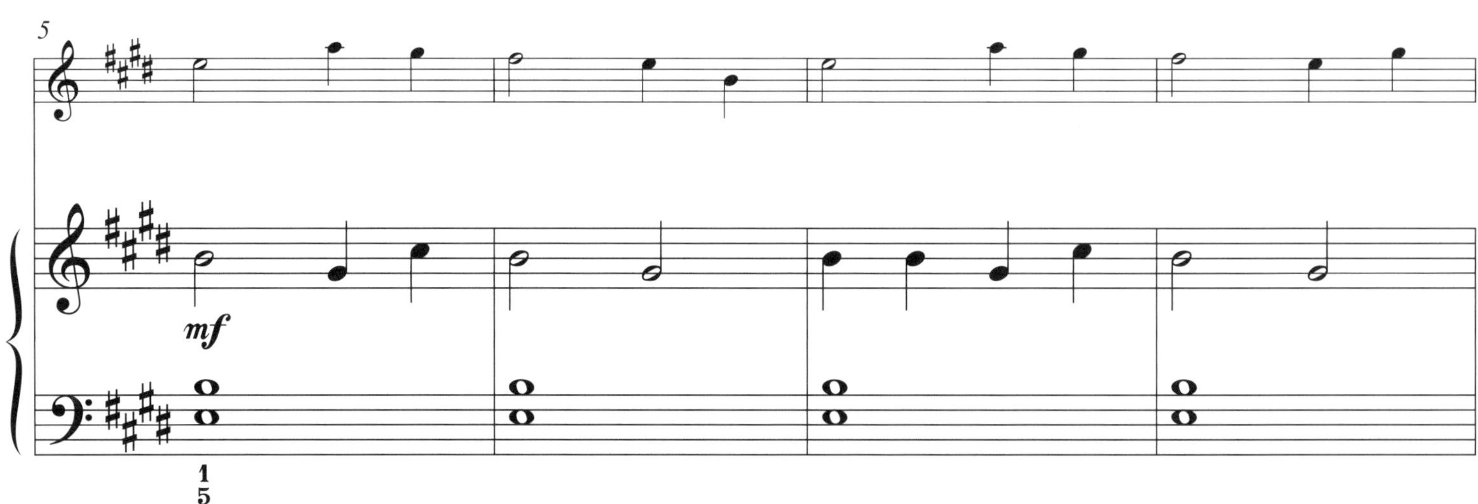

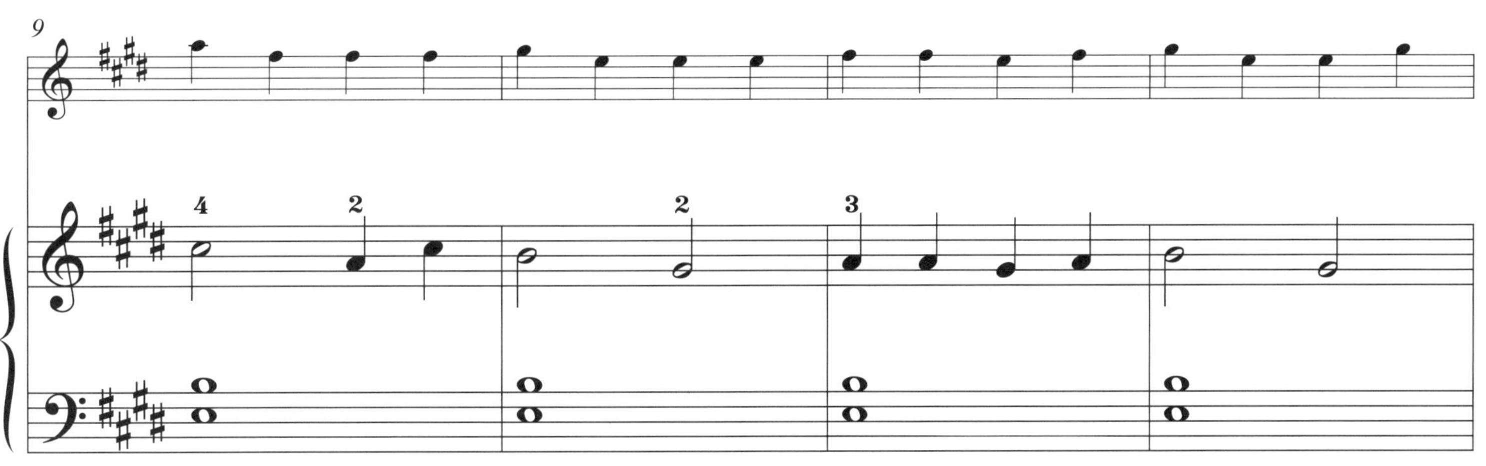
9
4
2
2
3

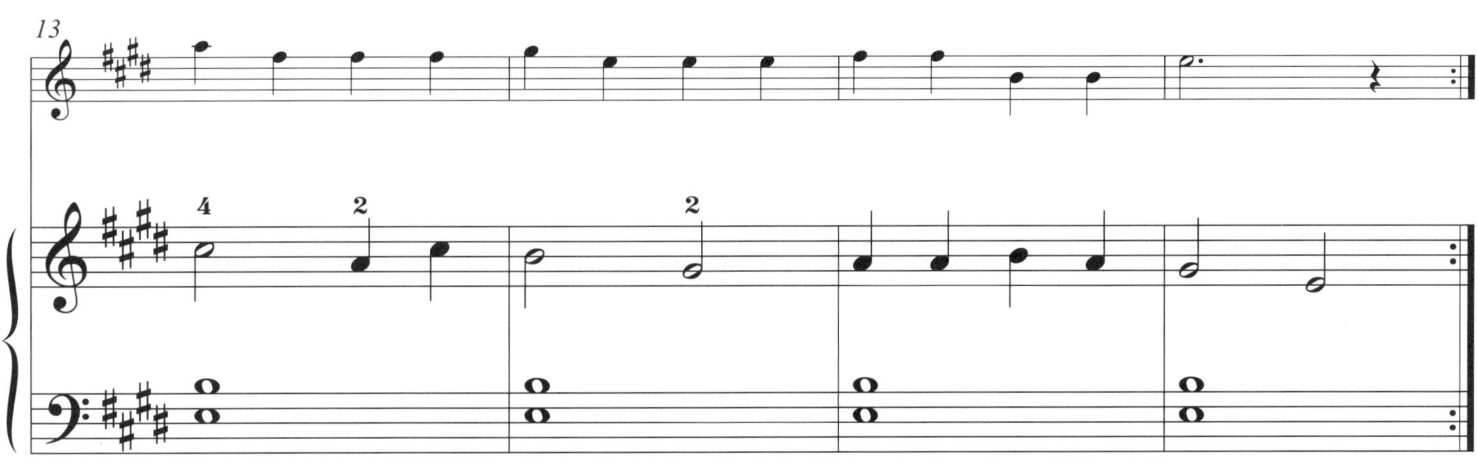
13
4
2
2

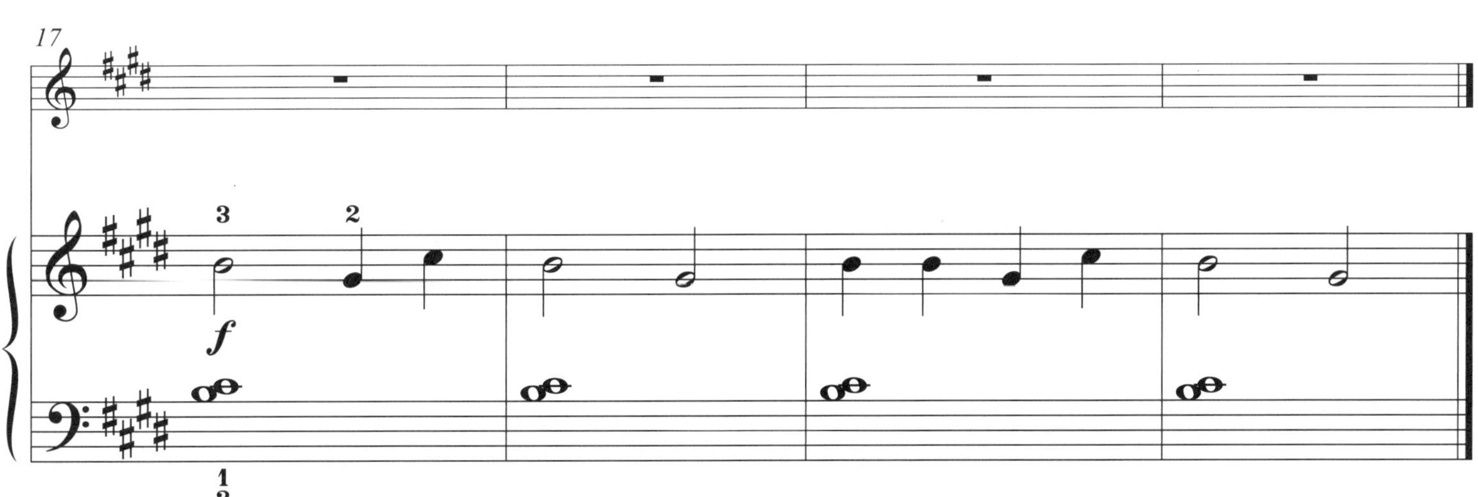
17
3
2
f
1
2

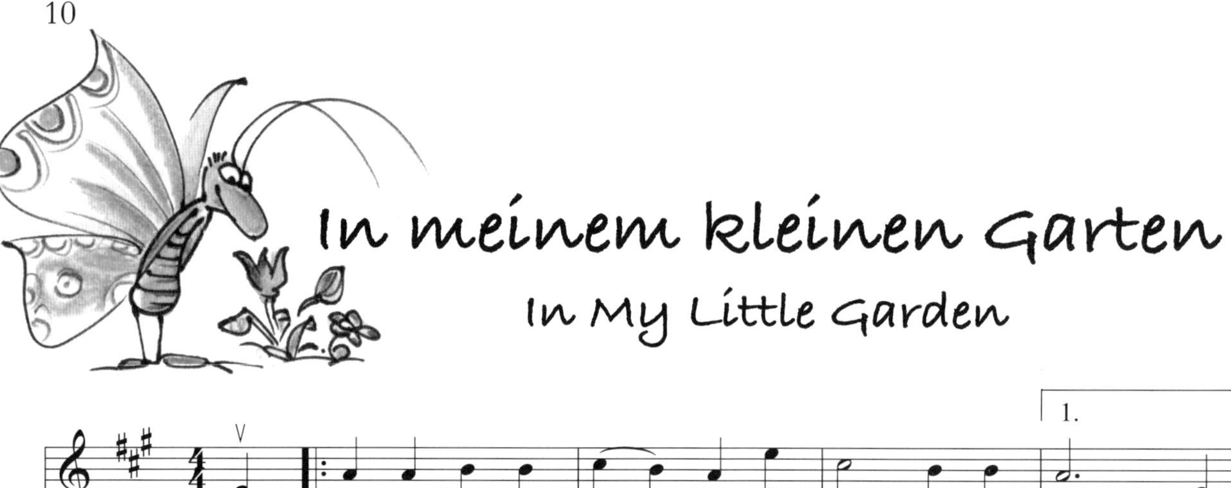

In meinem kleinen Garten

In My Little Garden

Karin Groß

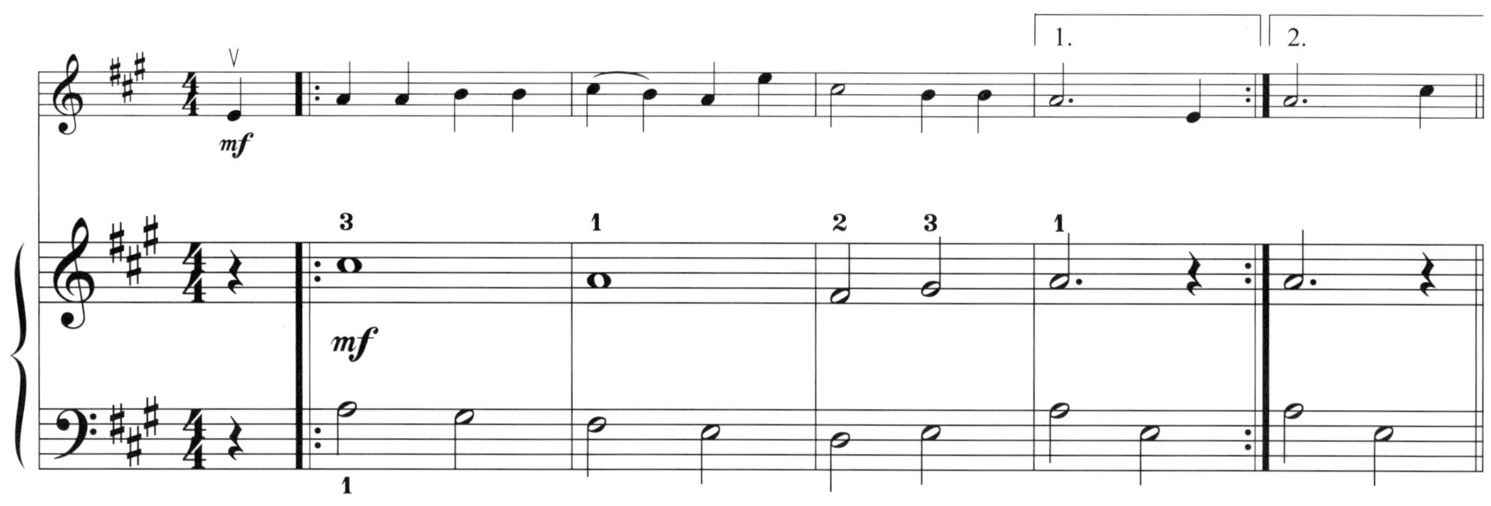

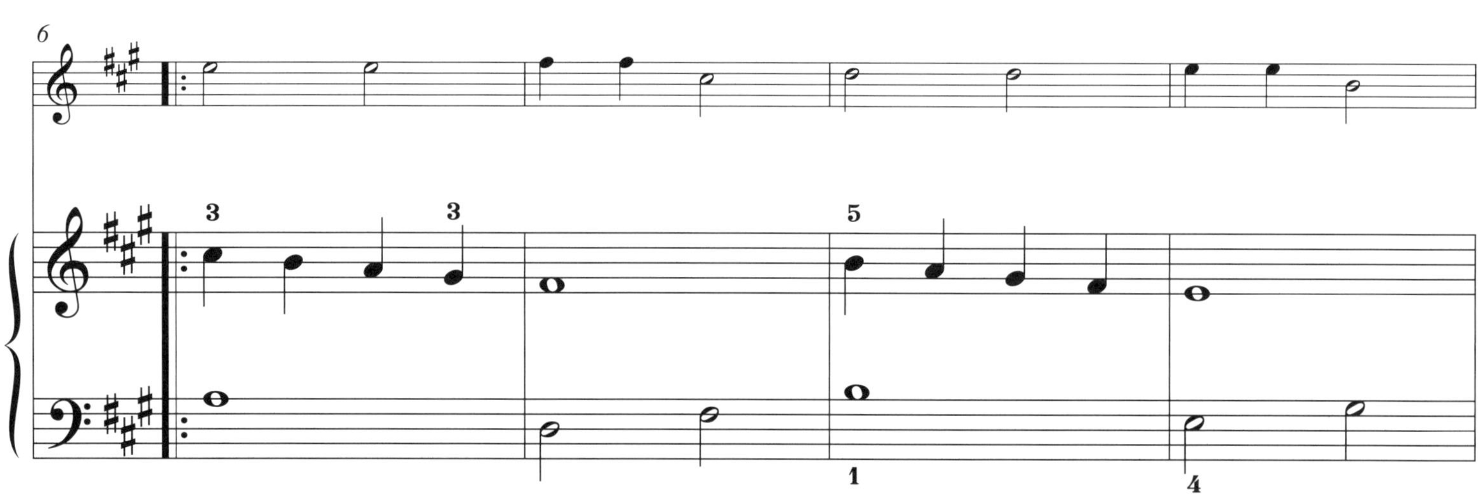

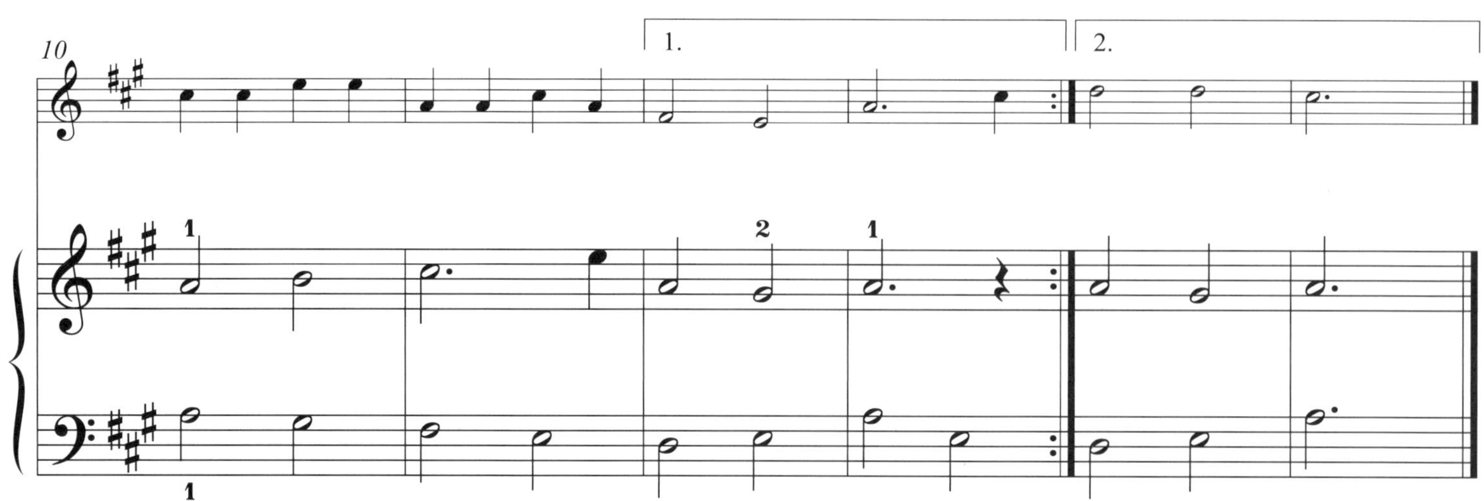

Abendstille

The Quiet Of The Evening

Mit großer Ruhe
With great calm

Karin Groß

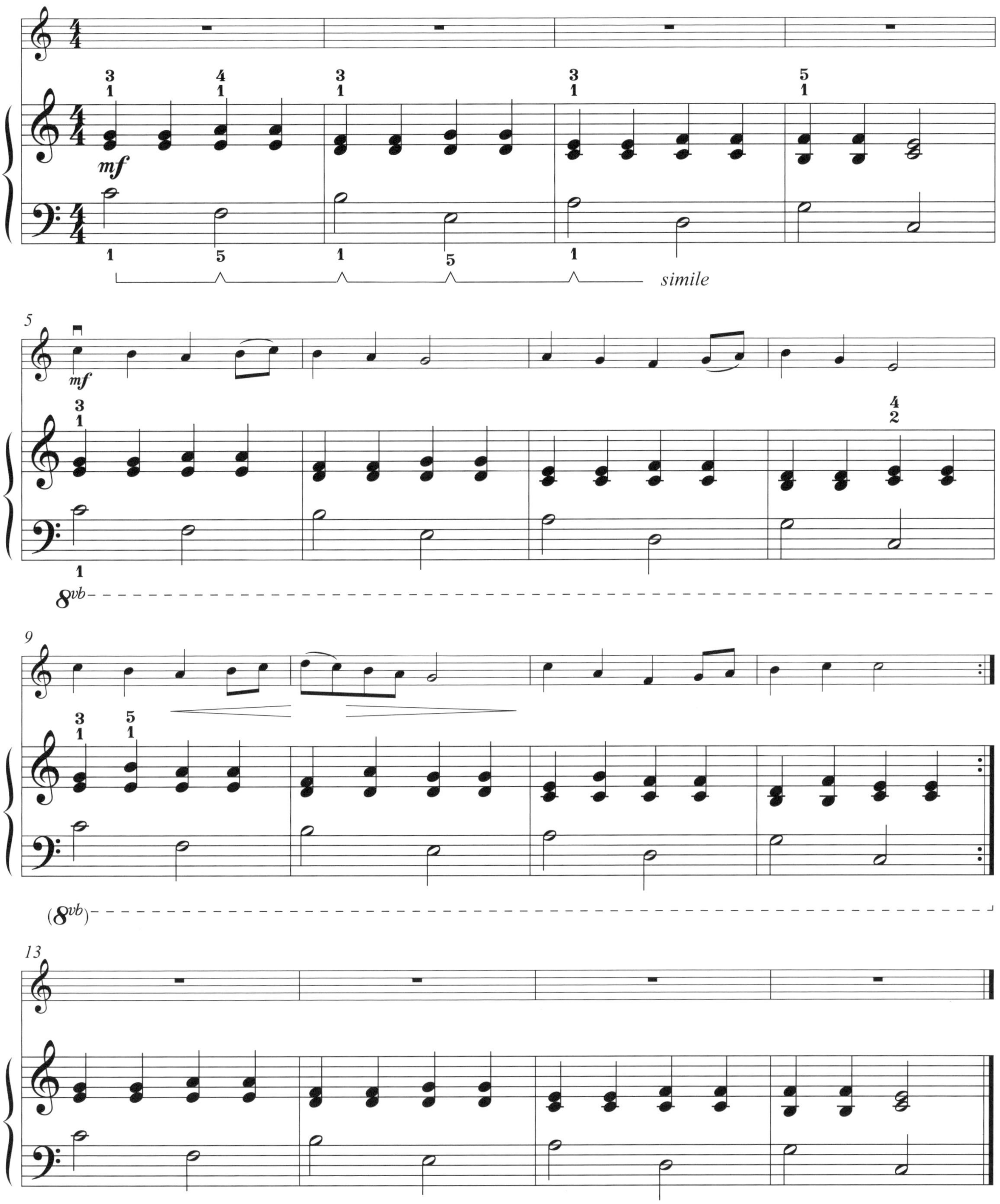

mf

simile

mf

8vb

(8vb)

Frühlingsboten

Harbingers Of Spring

Karin Groß

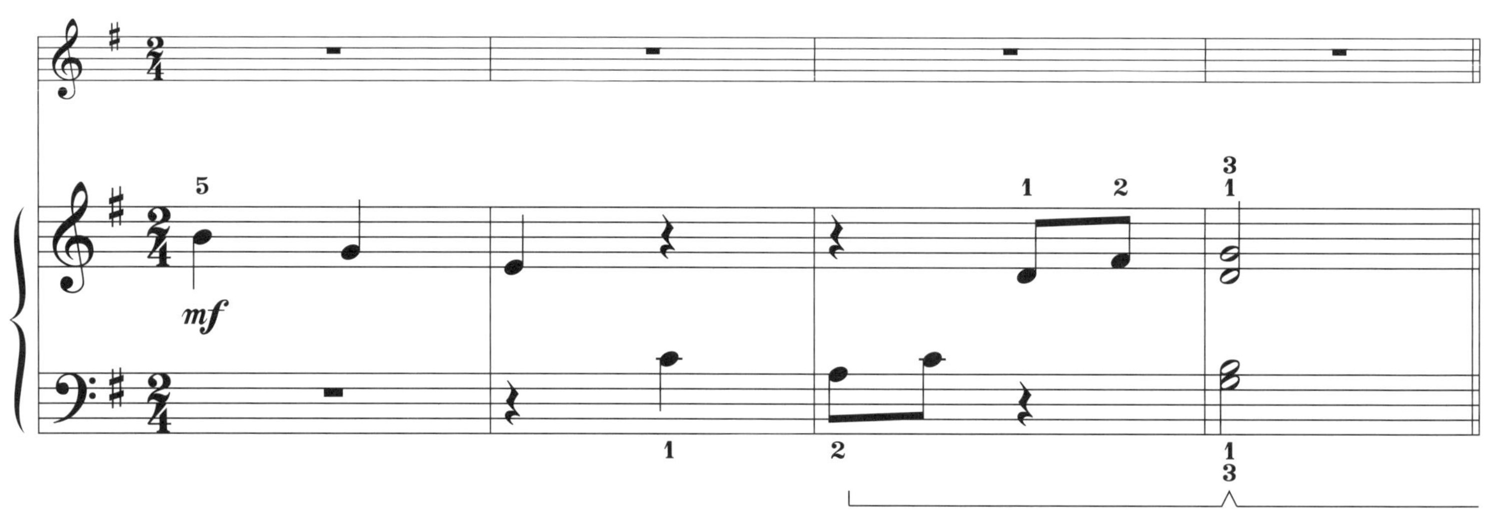

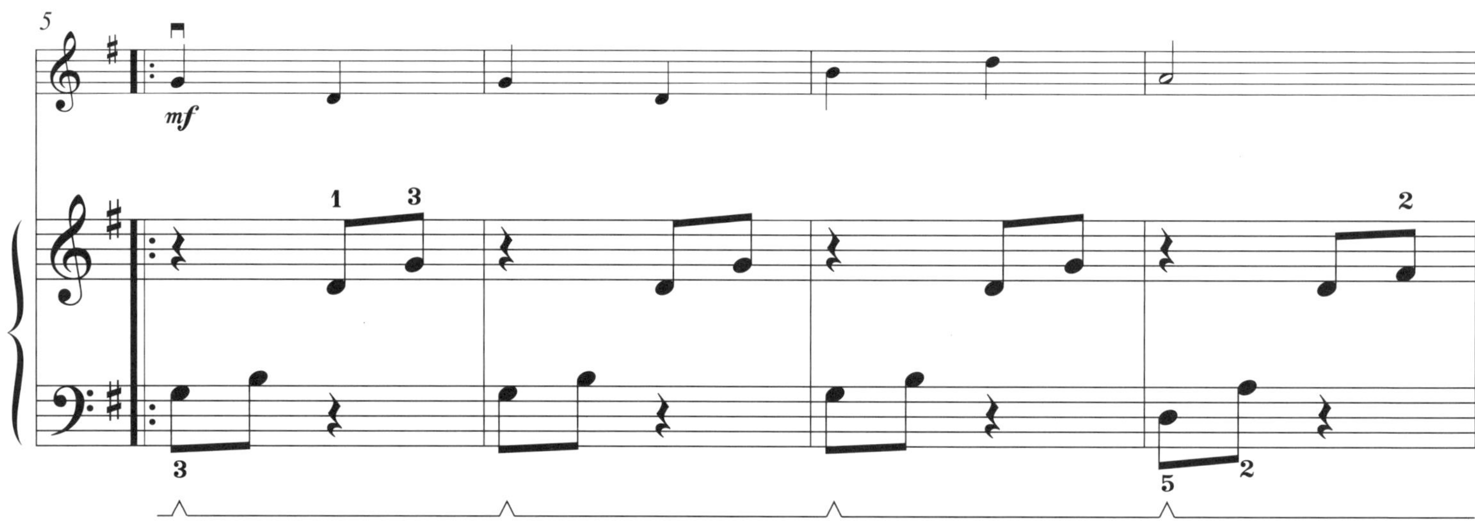

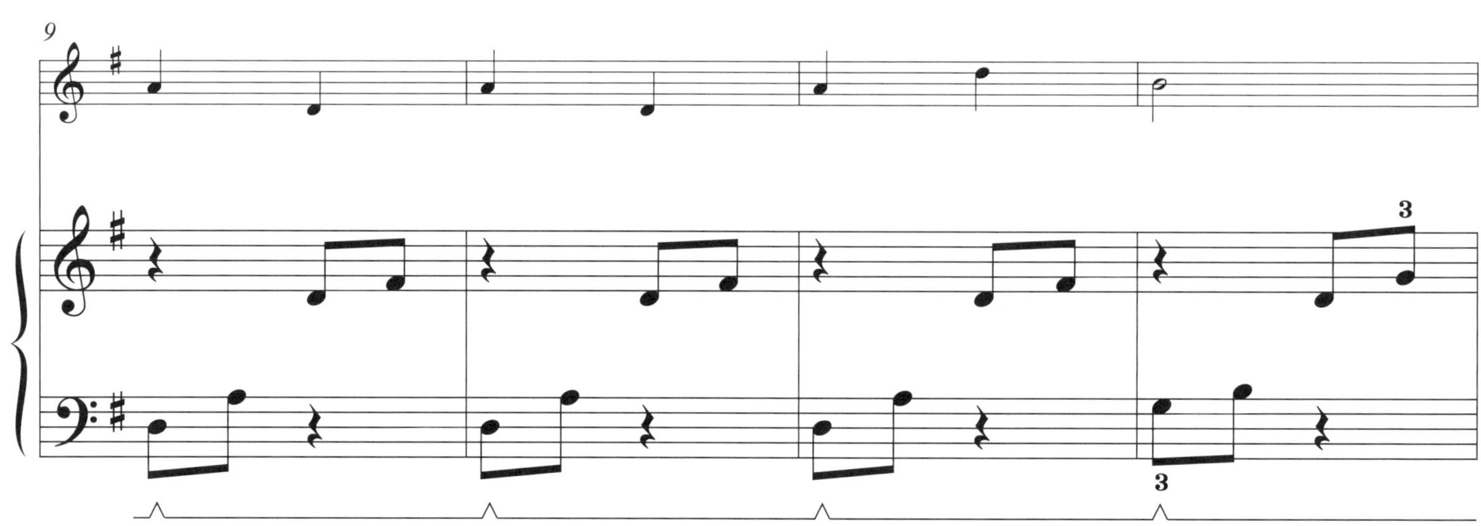

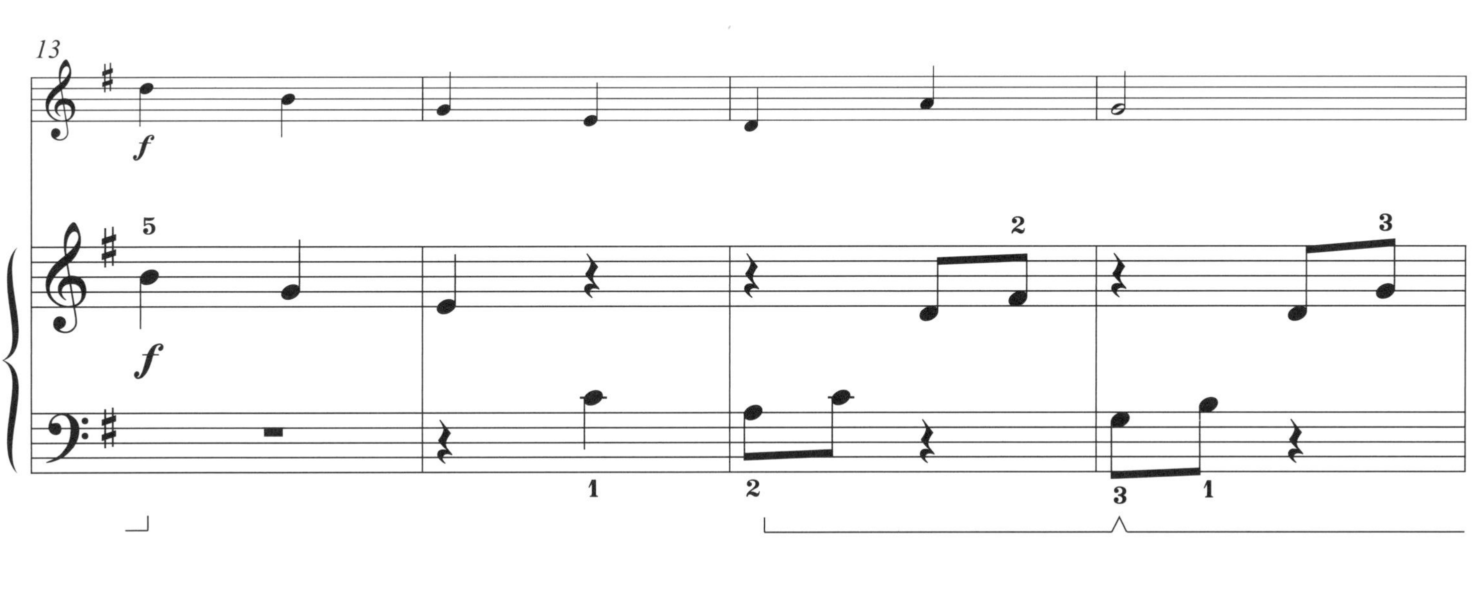

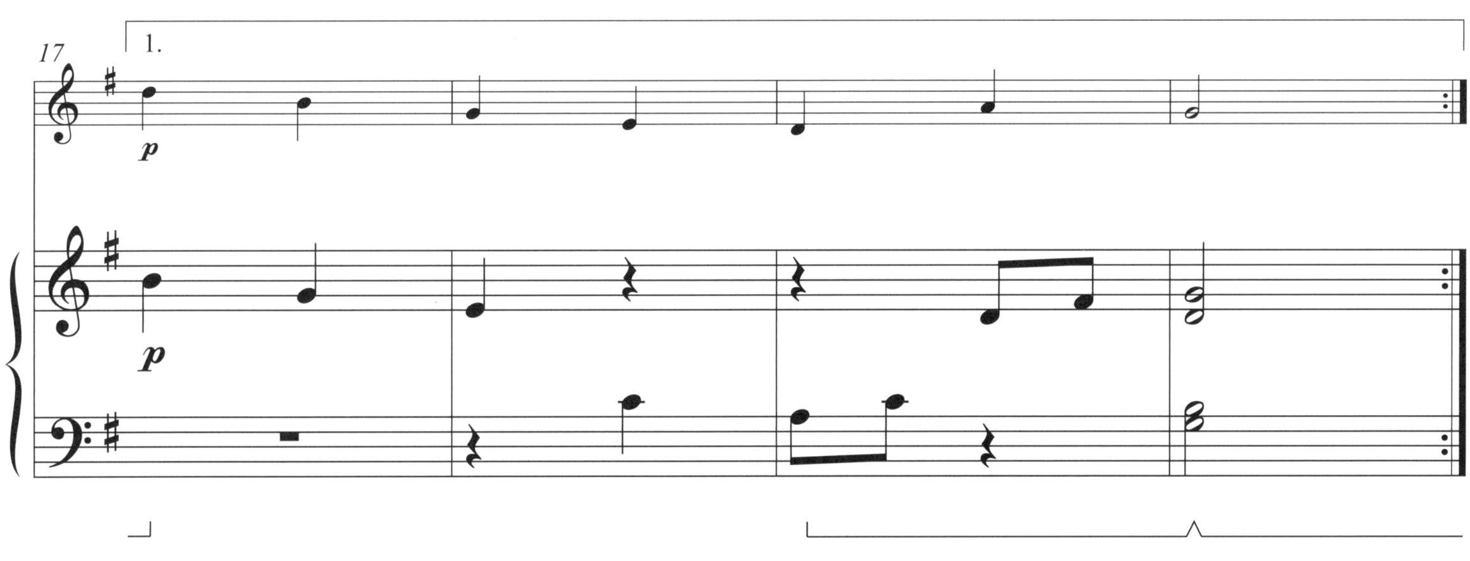
1.

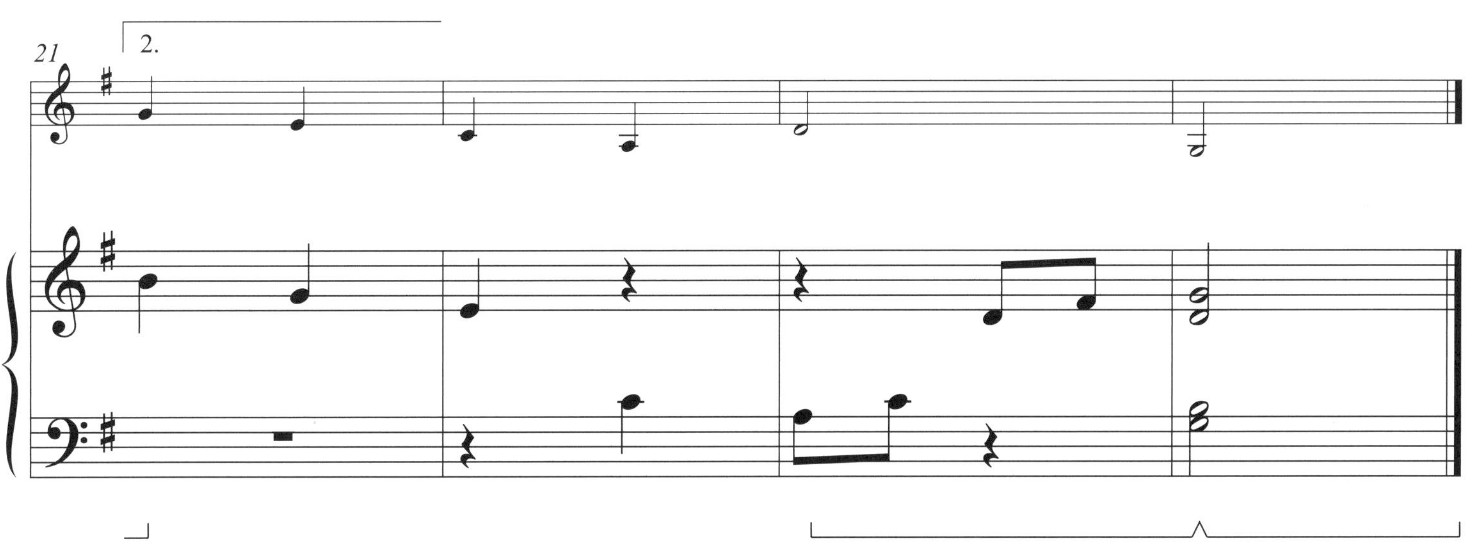
2.

Die Springmaus

The Jerboa

Lustig
Cheerfully

Karin Groß

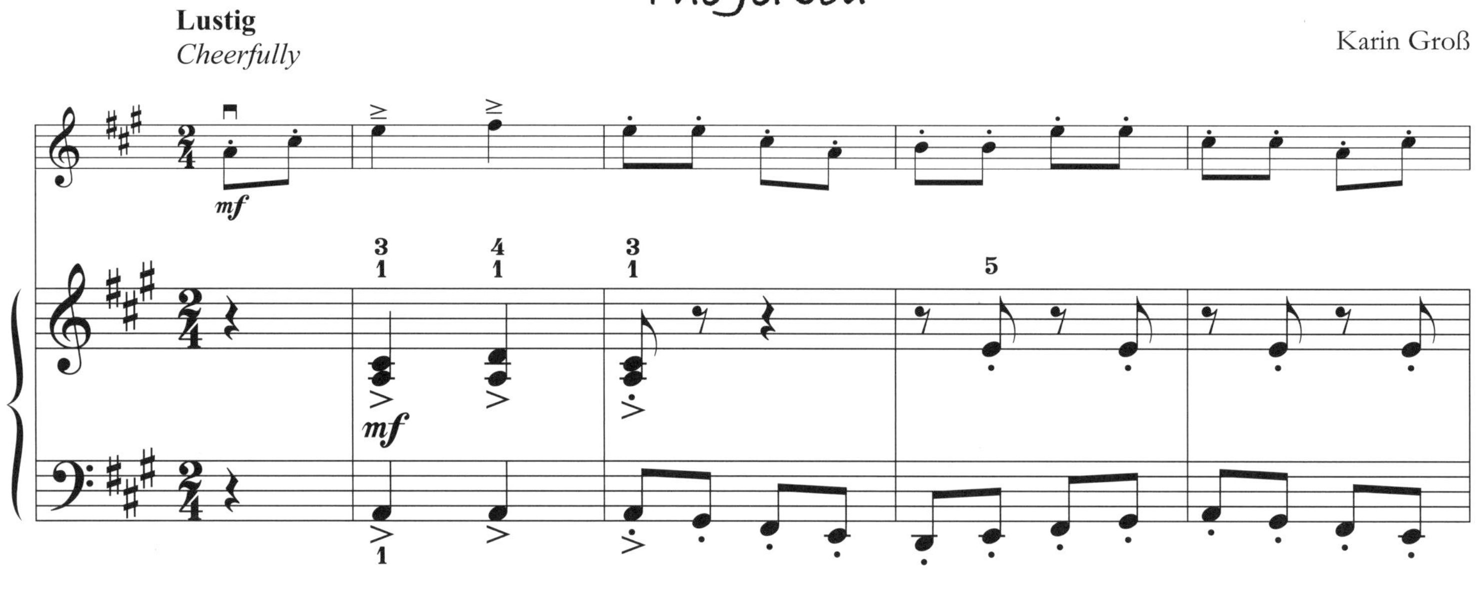

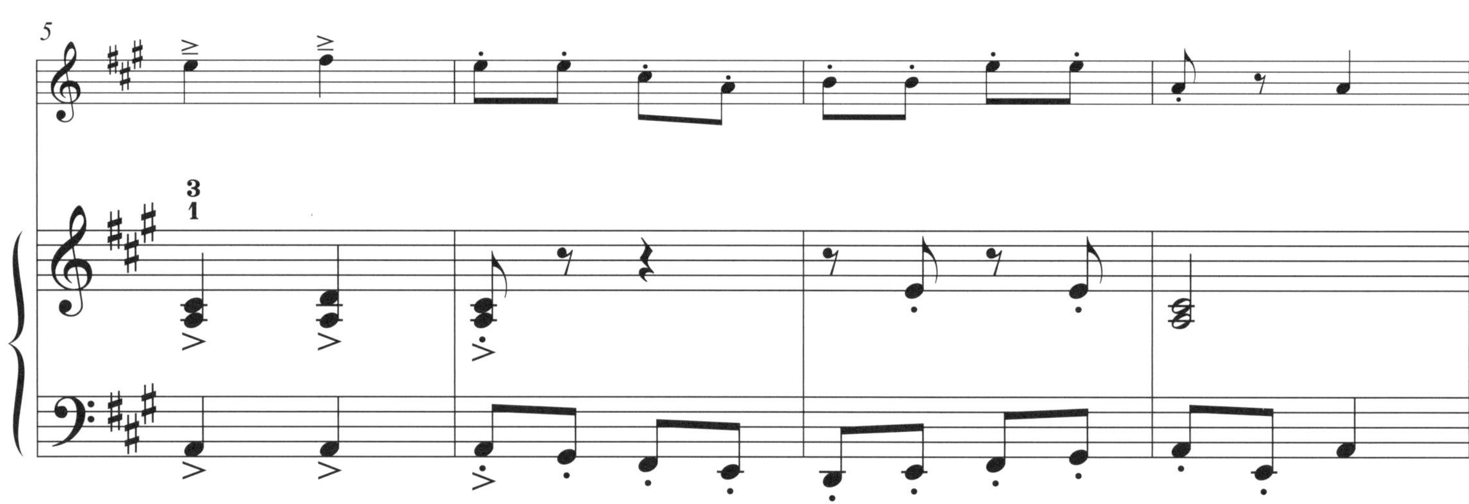

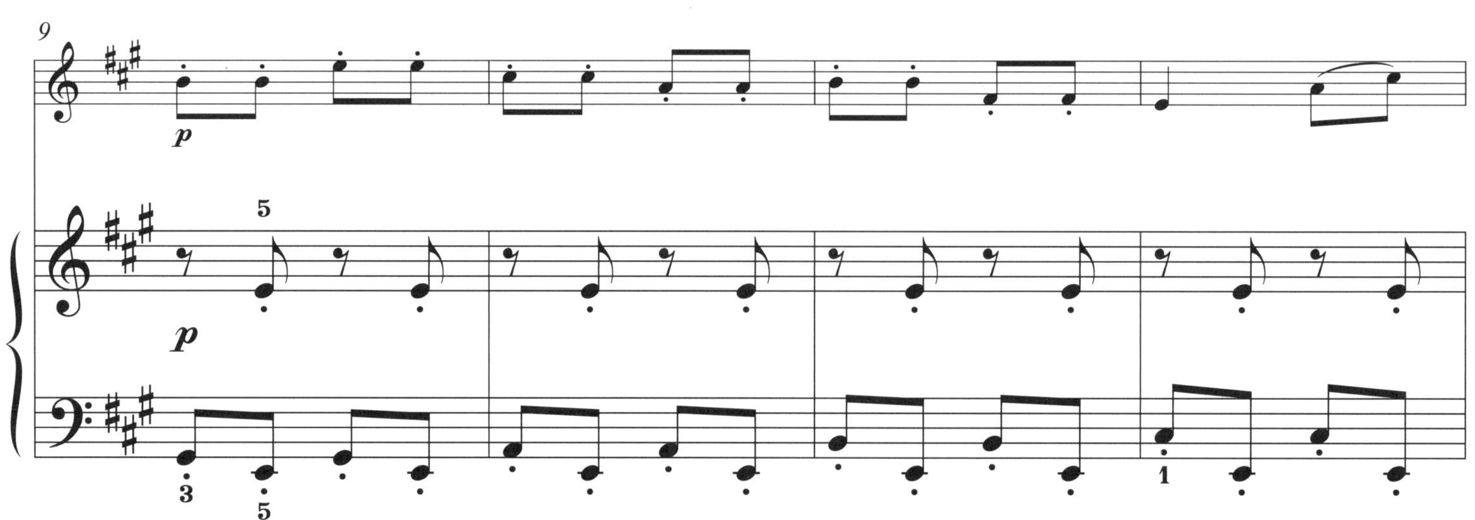

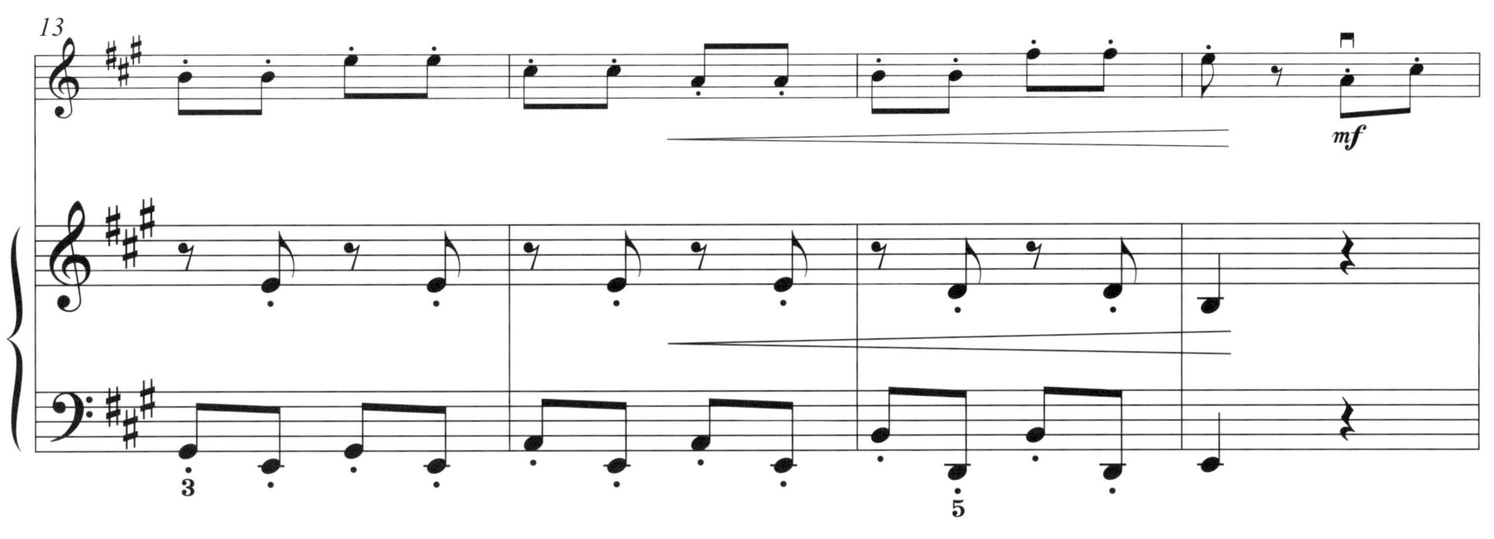
13
mf
3
5

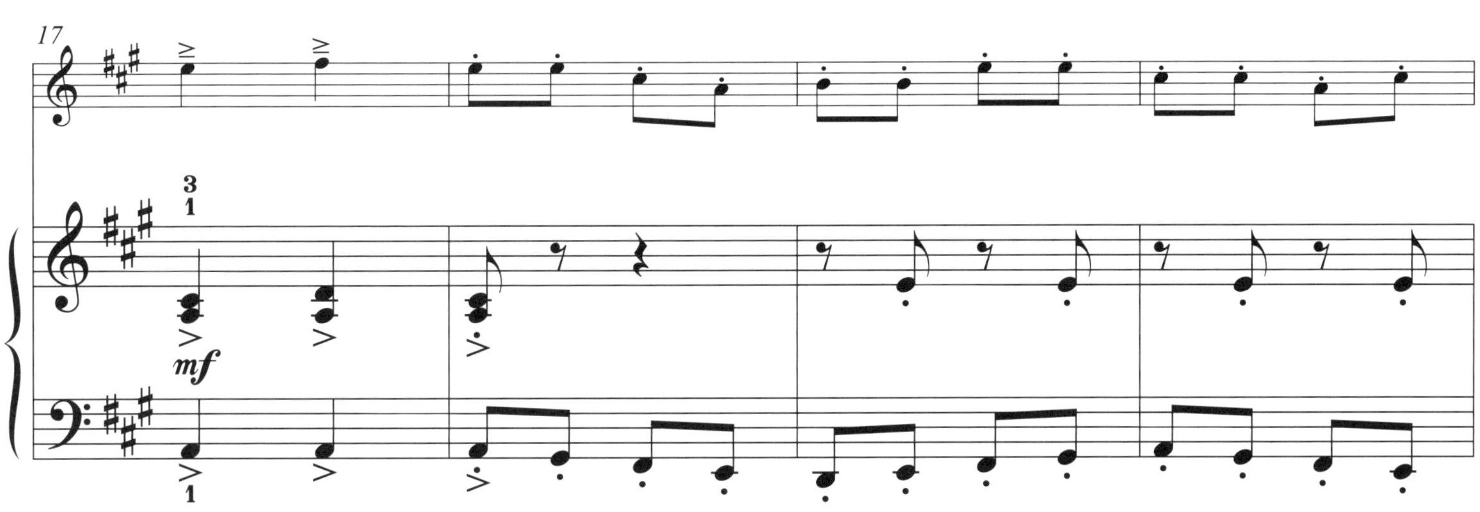
17
3
1
mf
1

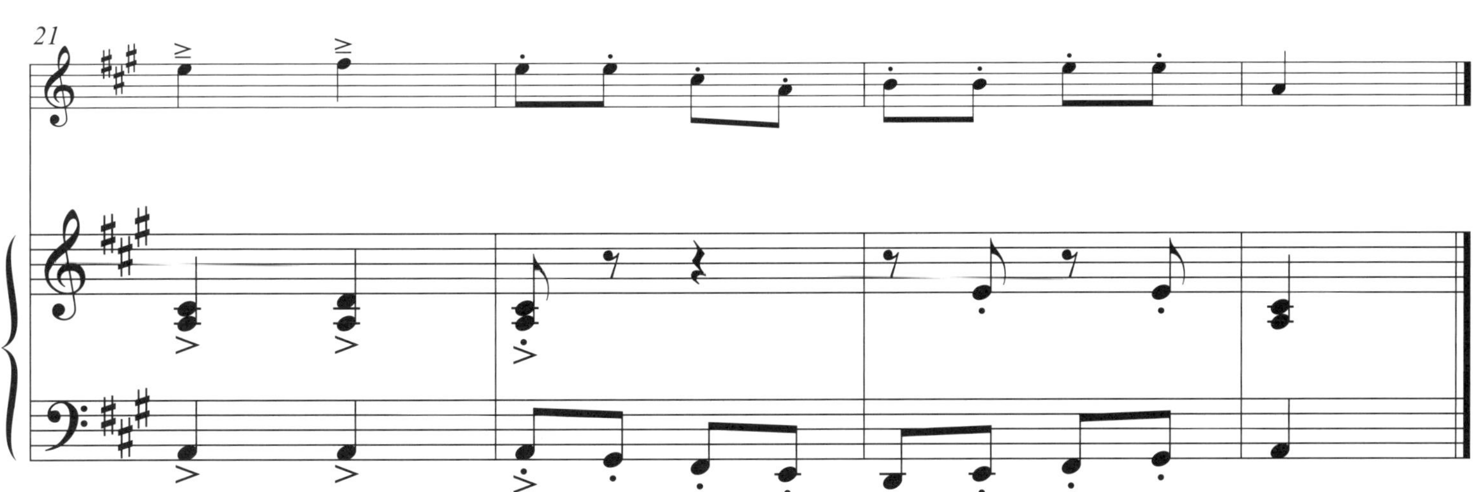
21

Abend in der Prärie

Evening In The Prairie

Friedvoll
Peacefully

Karin Groß

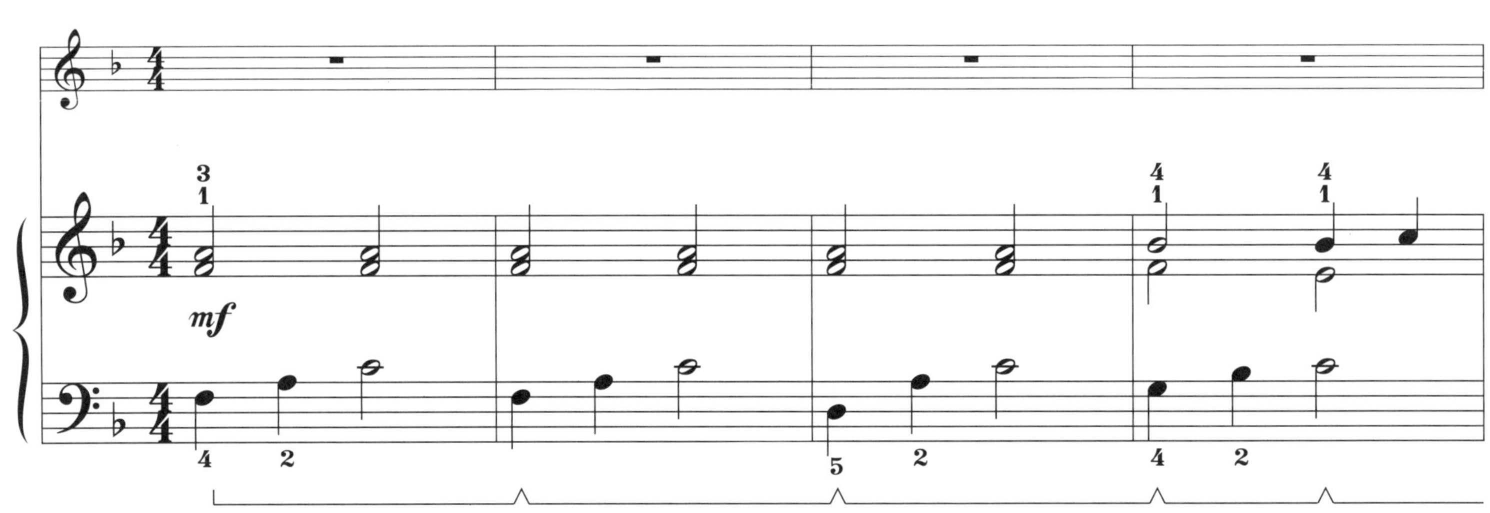

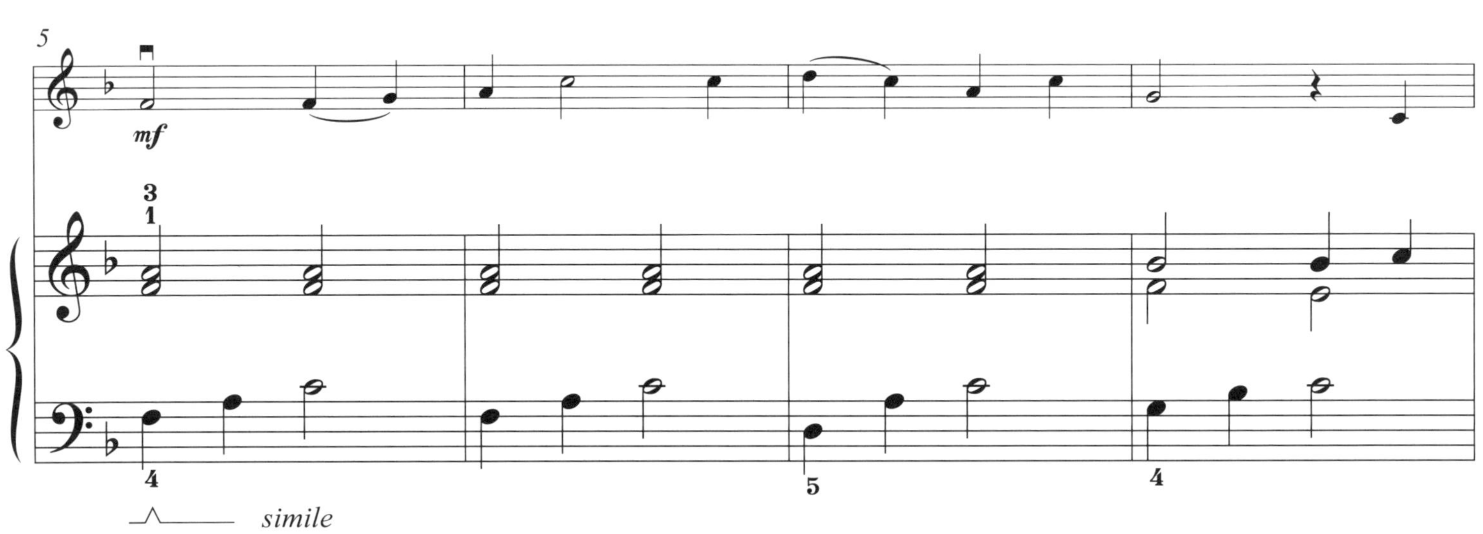

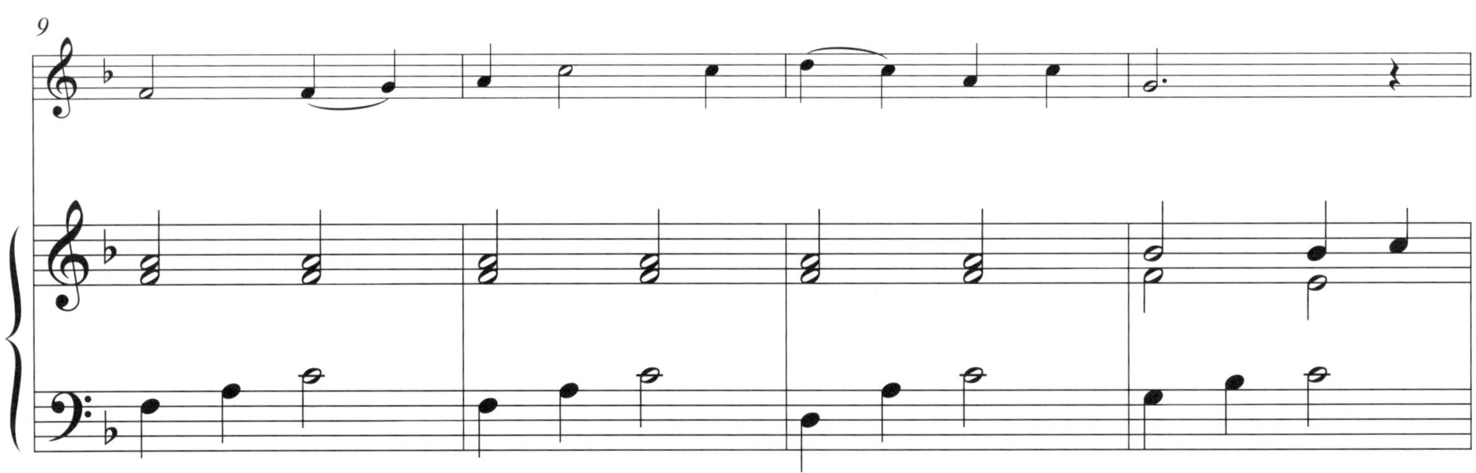

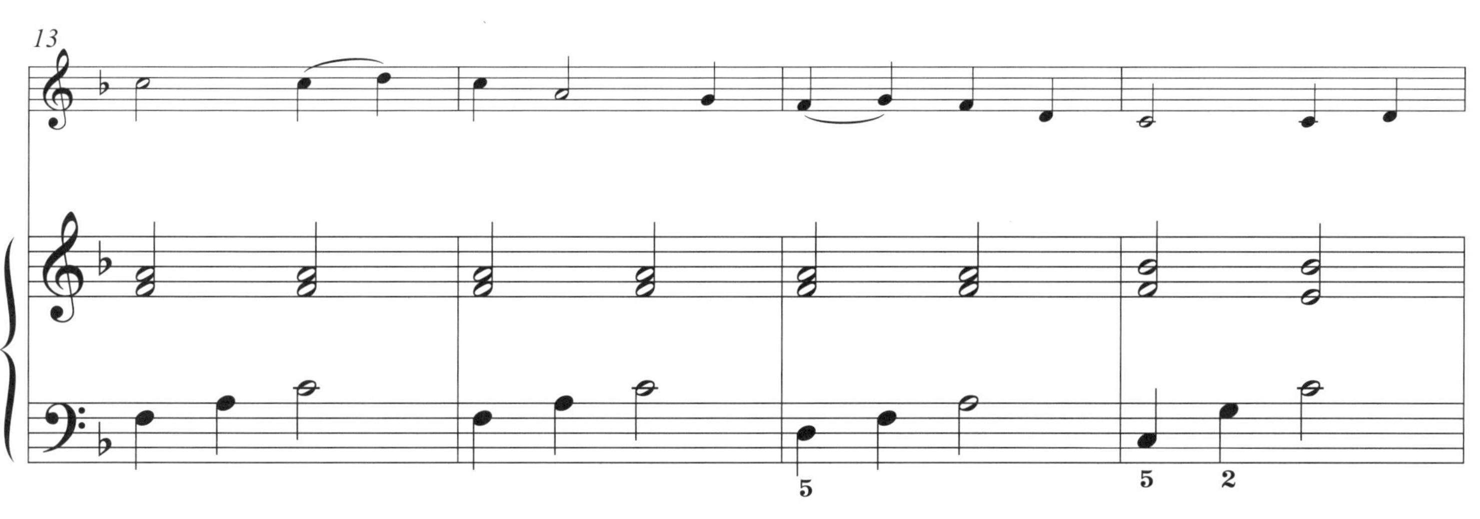

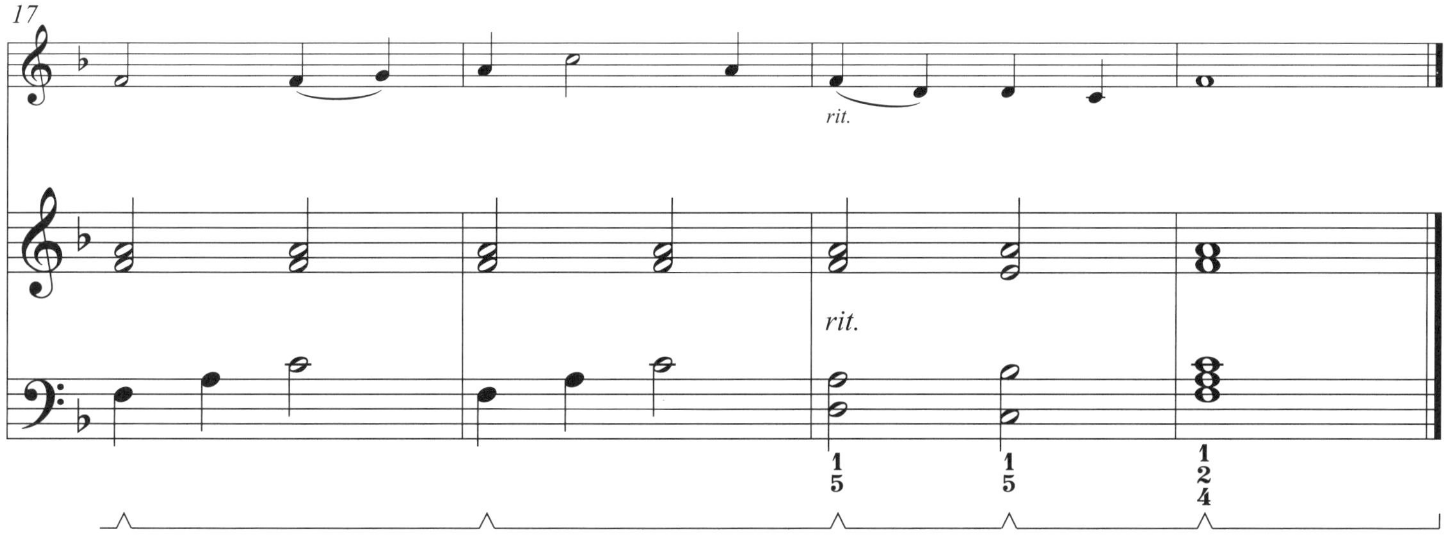

17

rit.

rit.

1 5 1 5 1 2 4

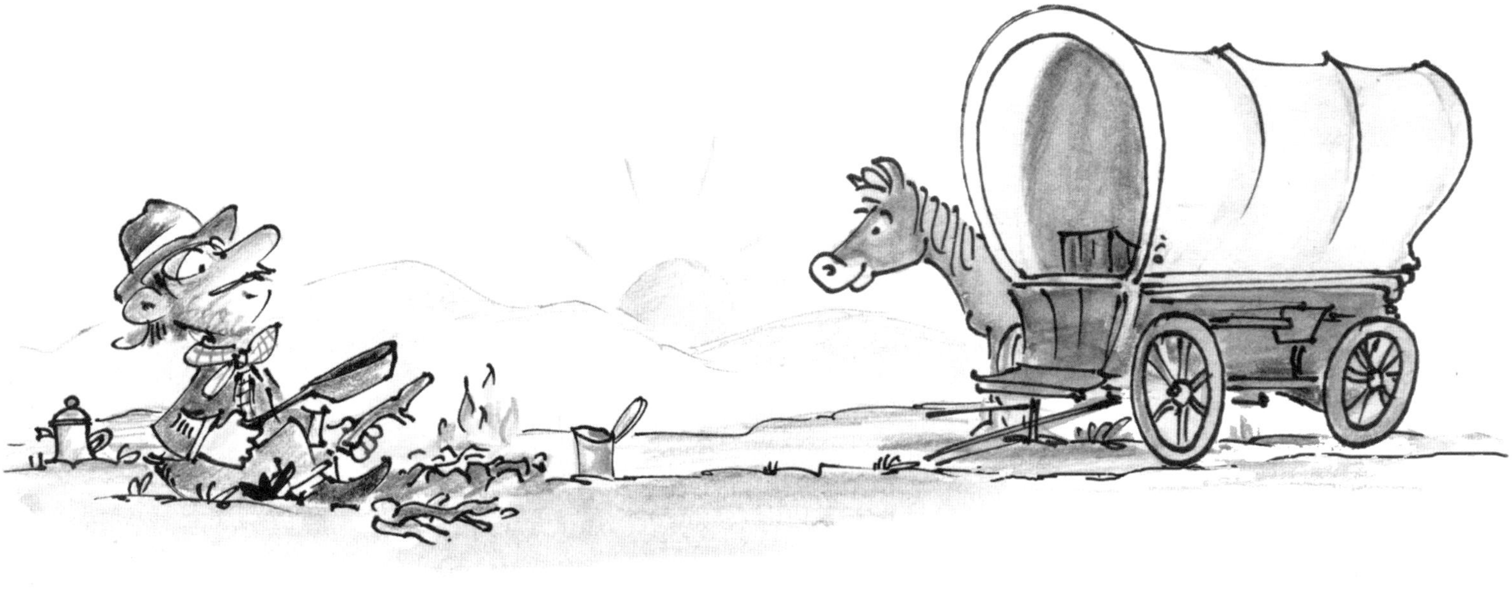

Opas Gute-Nacht-Geschichte

Grandad's Bedtime Story

Karin Groß

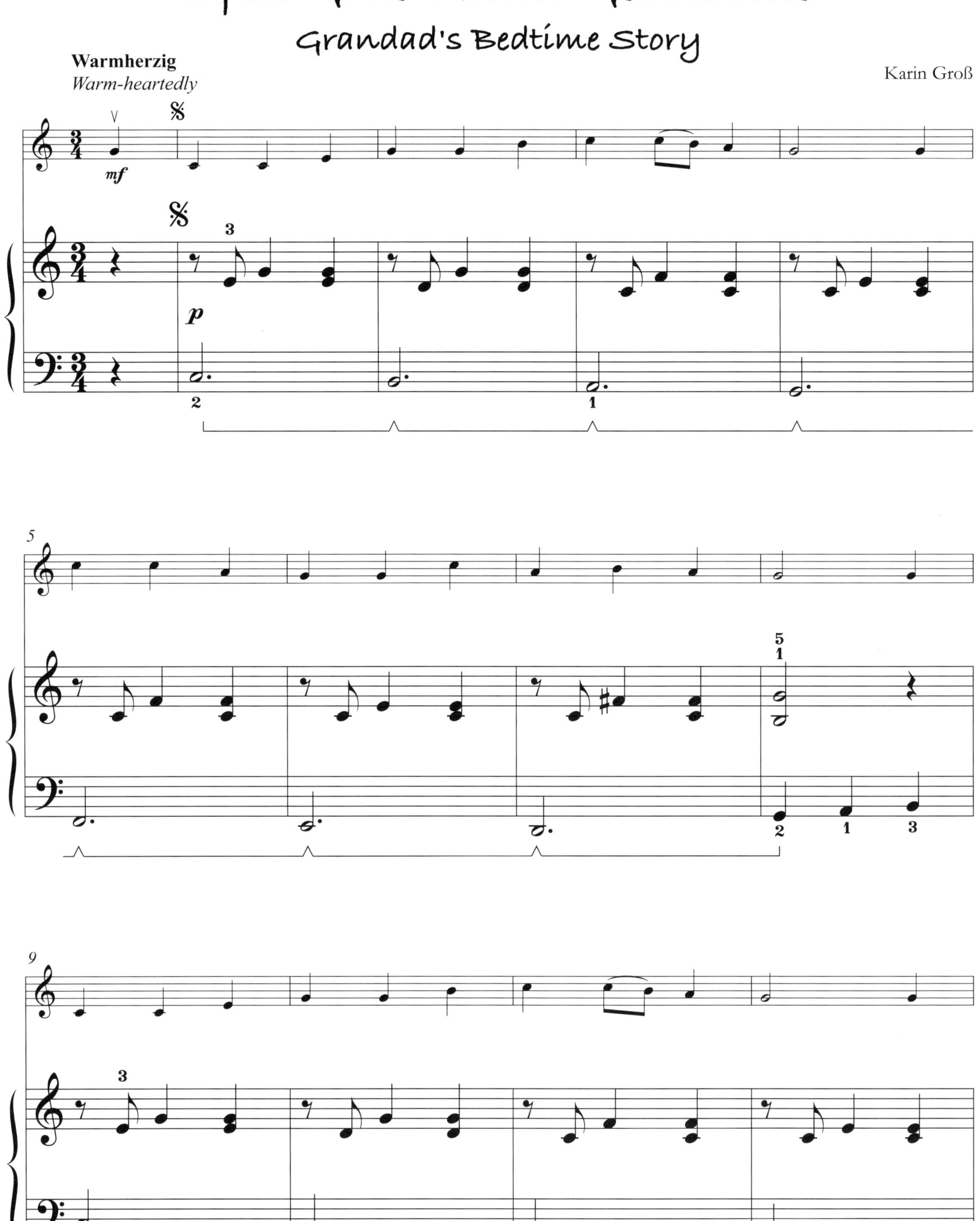

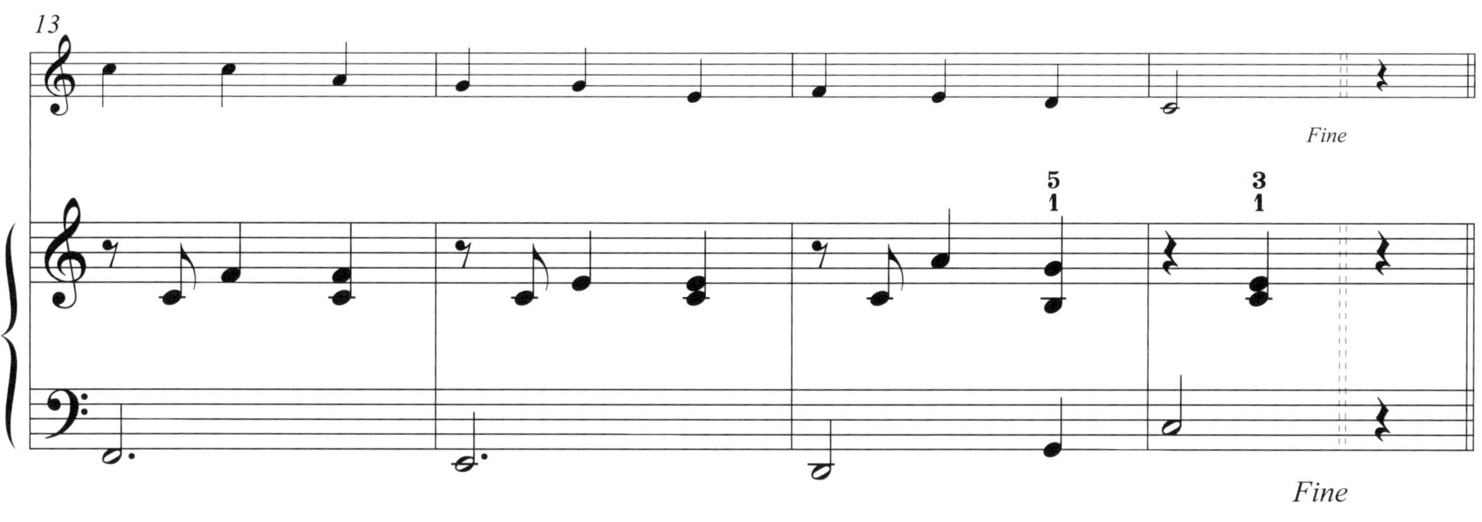
13
Fine
5
1
3
1
Fine

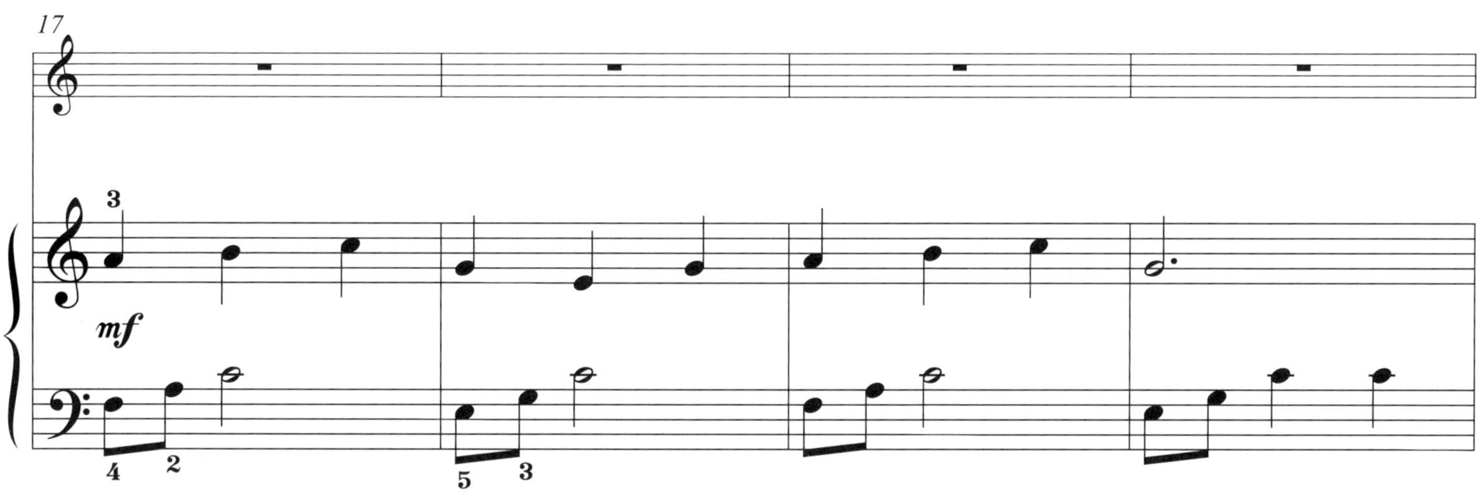
17
3
mf
4
2
5
3

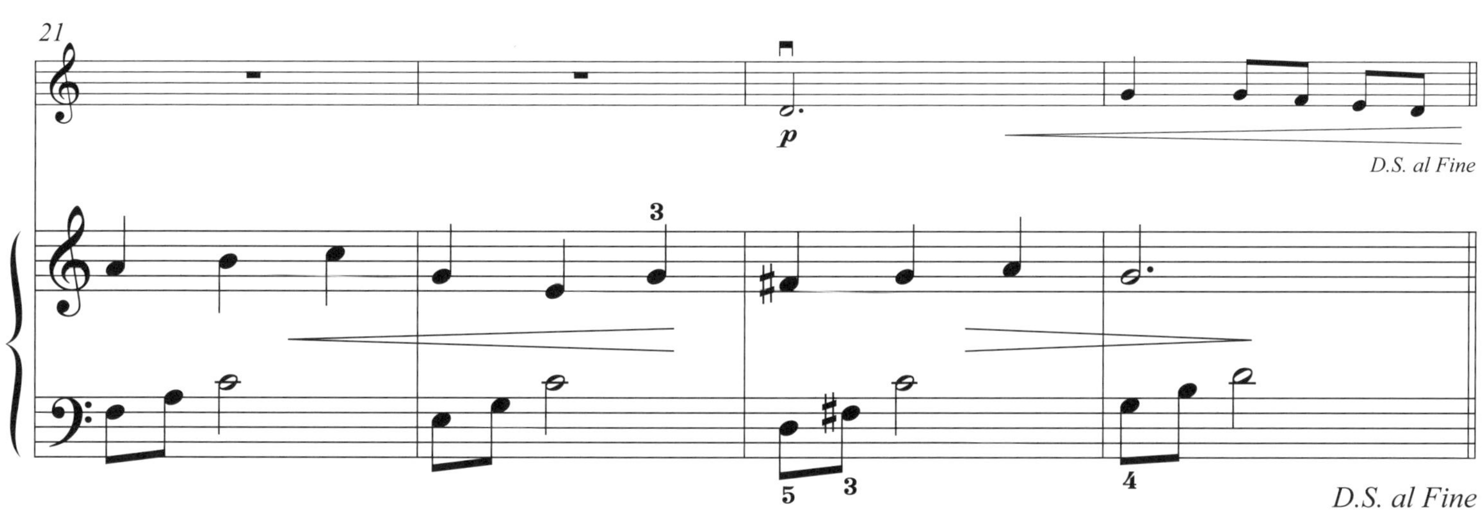
21
p
D.S. al Fine
3
5
3
4
D.S. al Fine

Pandabärs Fest

Panda's Party

Gemütlich
Leisurely

Karin Groß

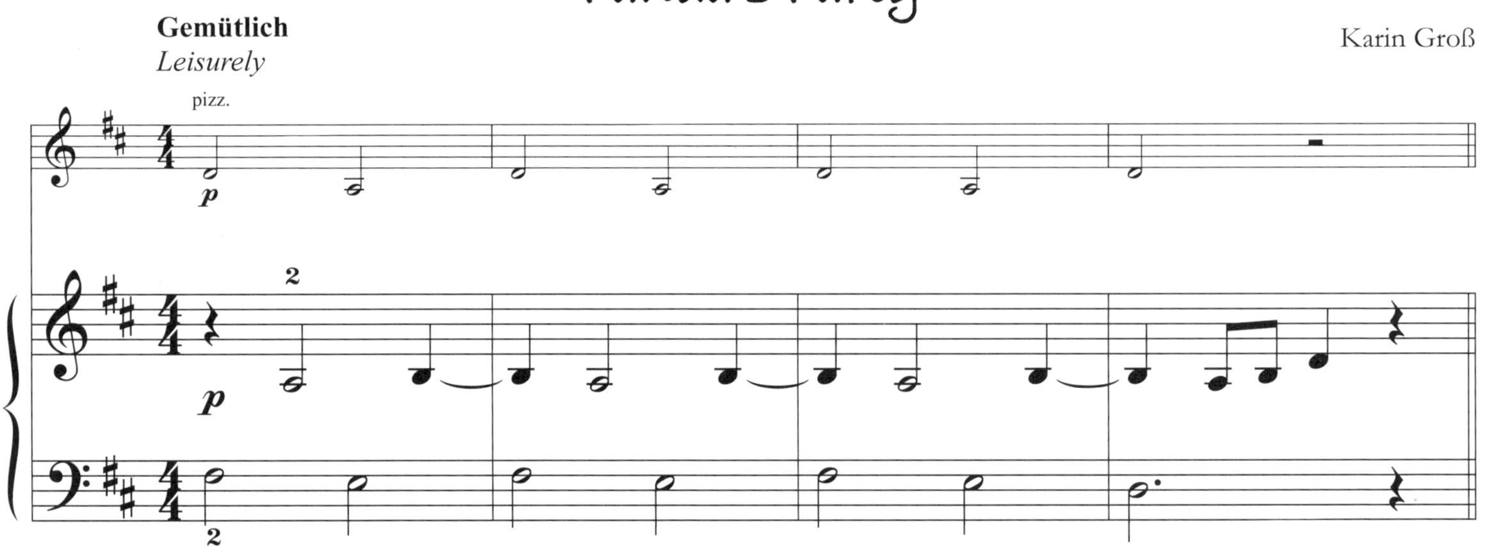

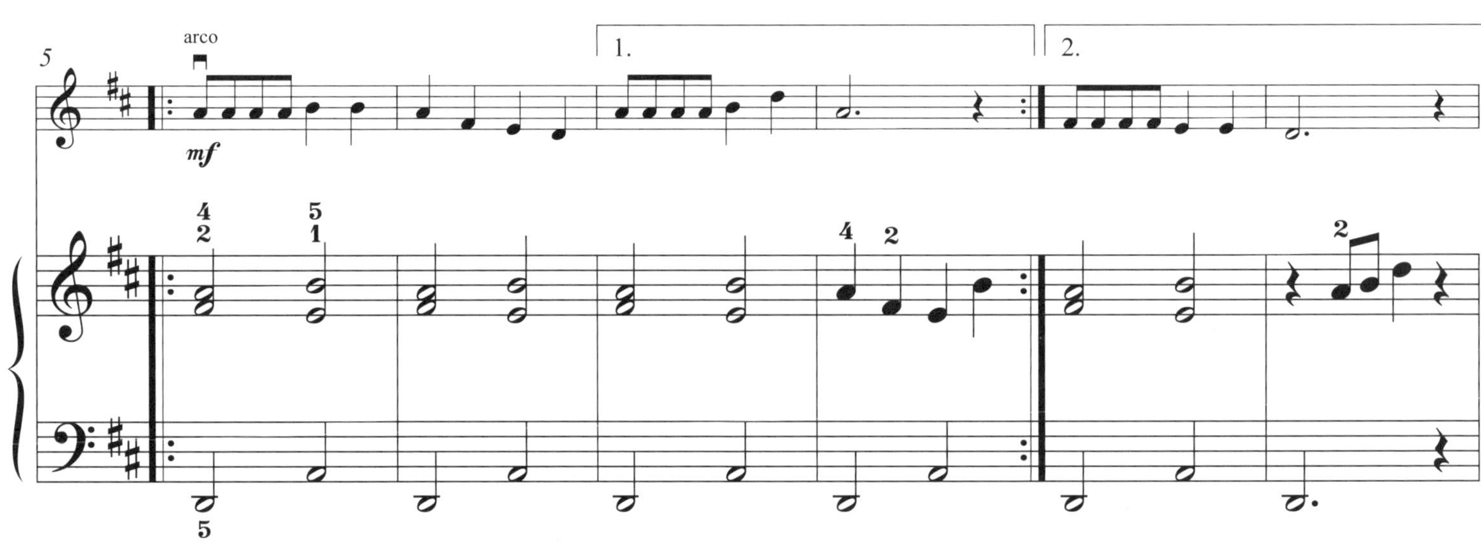

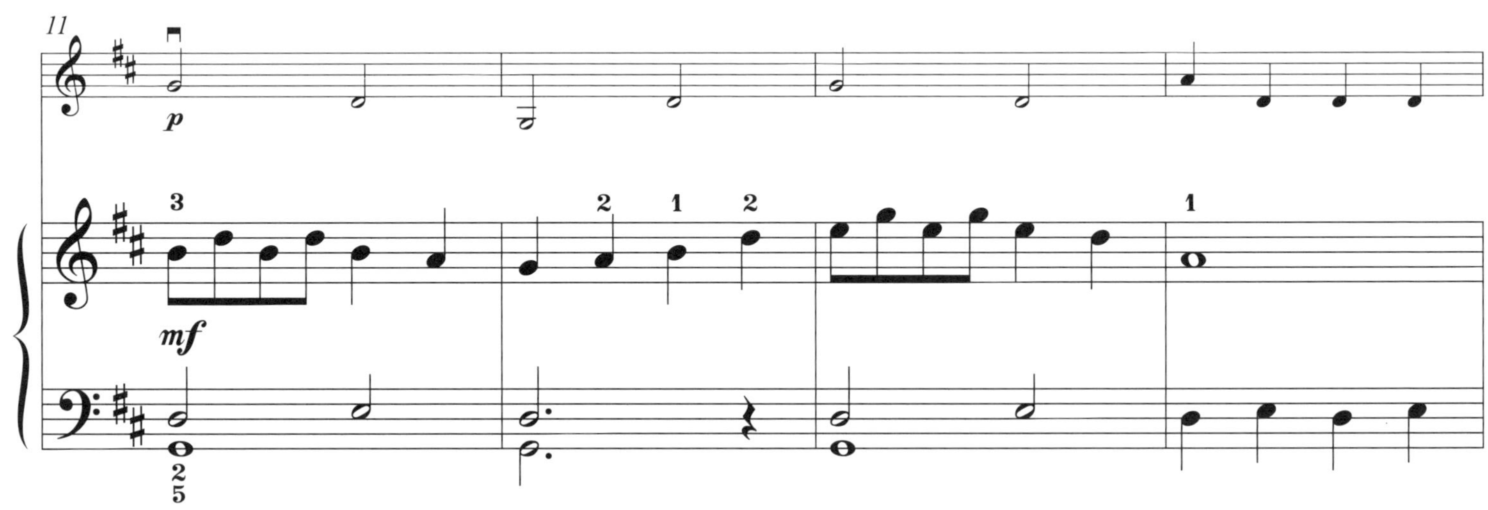

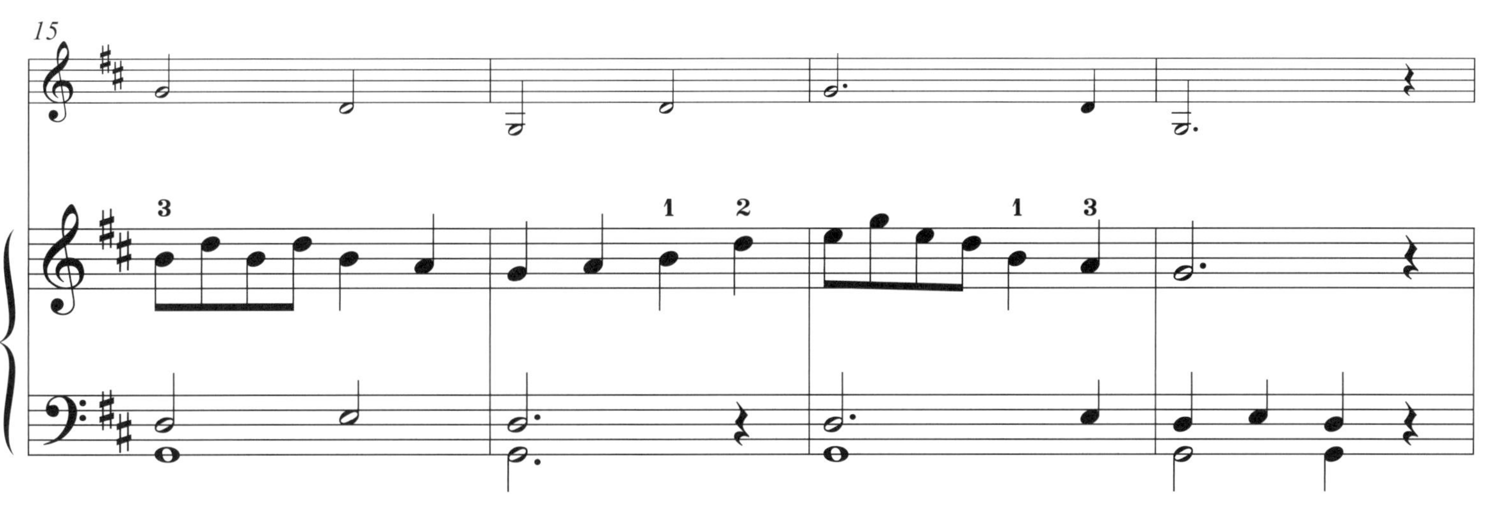
15
3
1
2
1
3

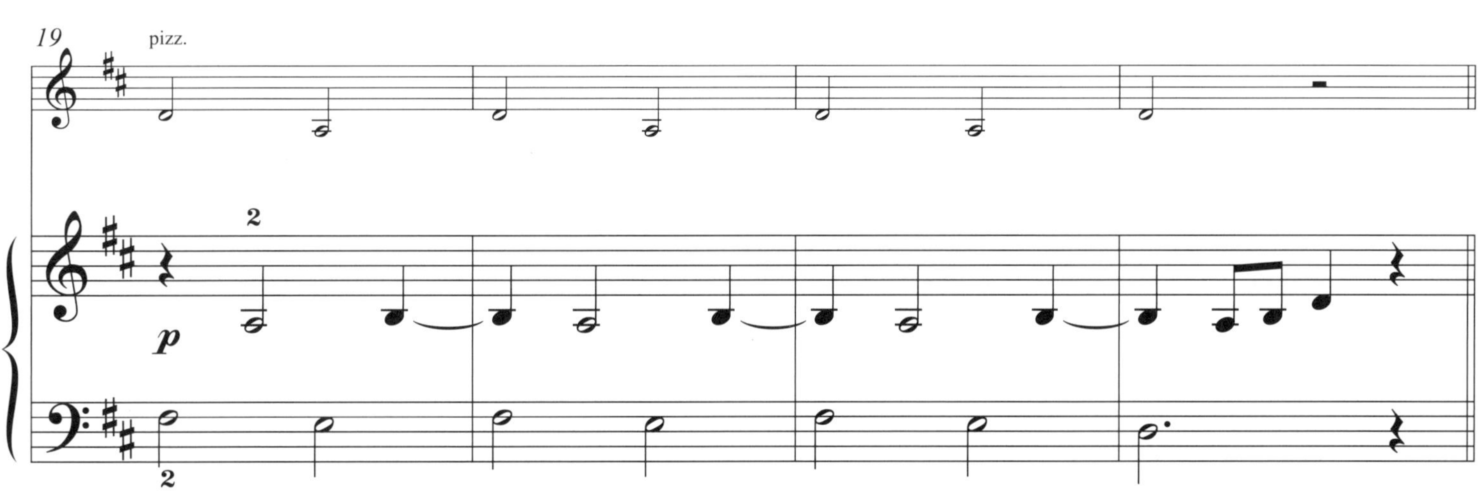
19
pizz.
2
p
2

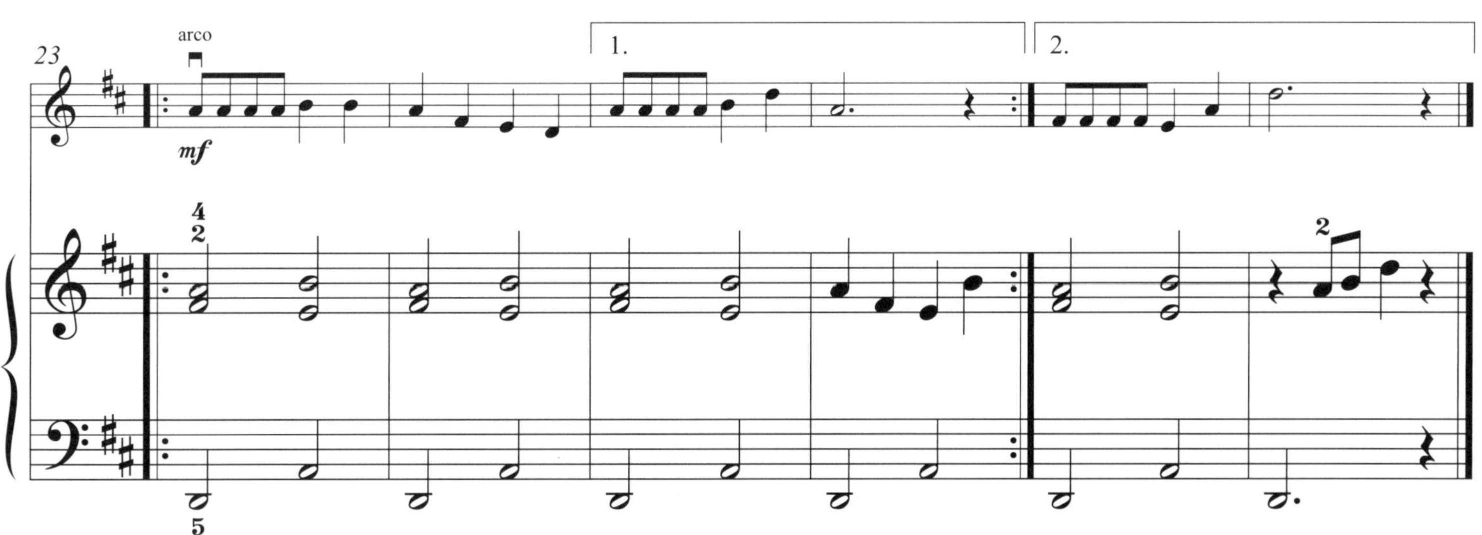
23
arco
mf
1.
2.
4
2
2
5

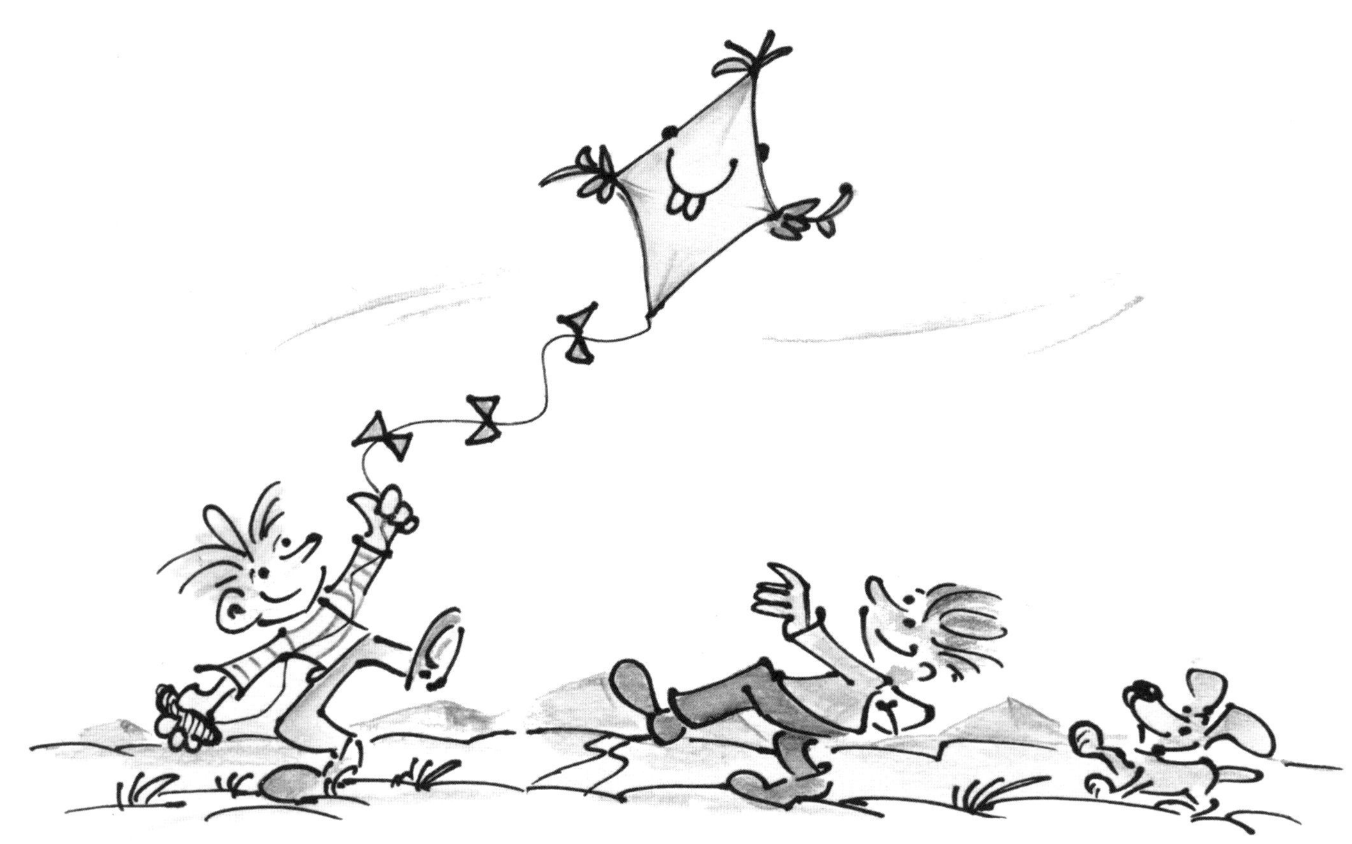

Drachenflug

Flying Kites

Gleitend
As if gliding

Karin Groß

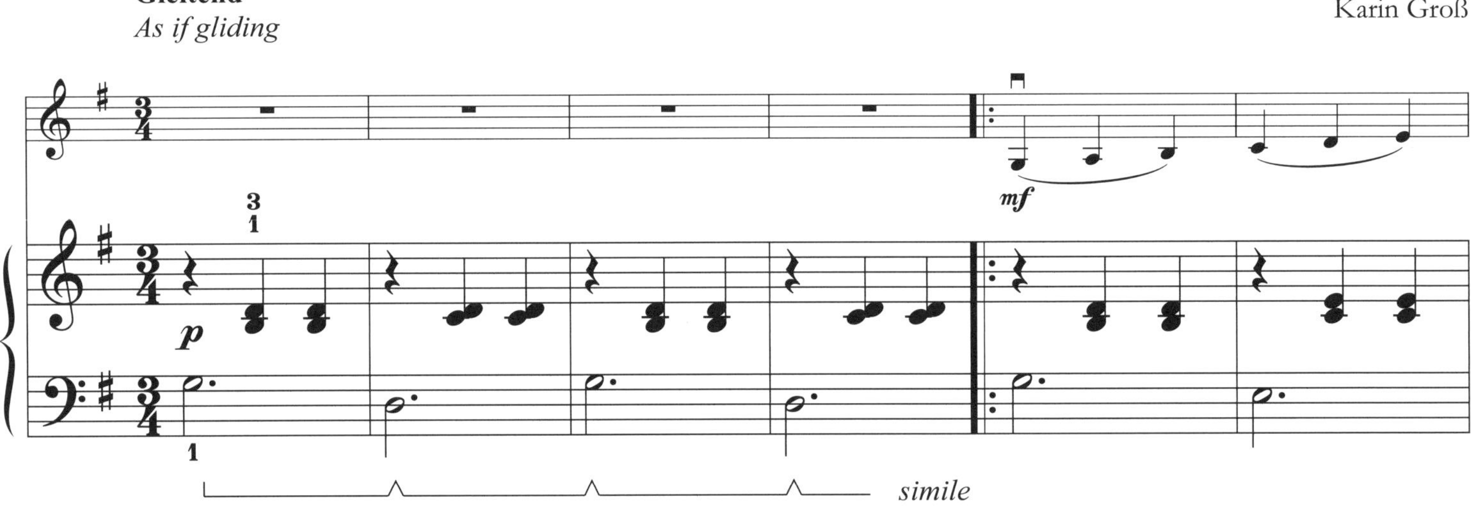

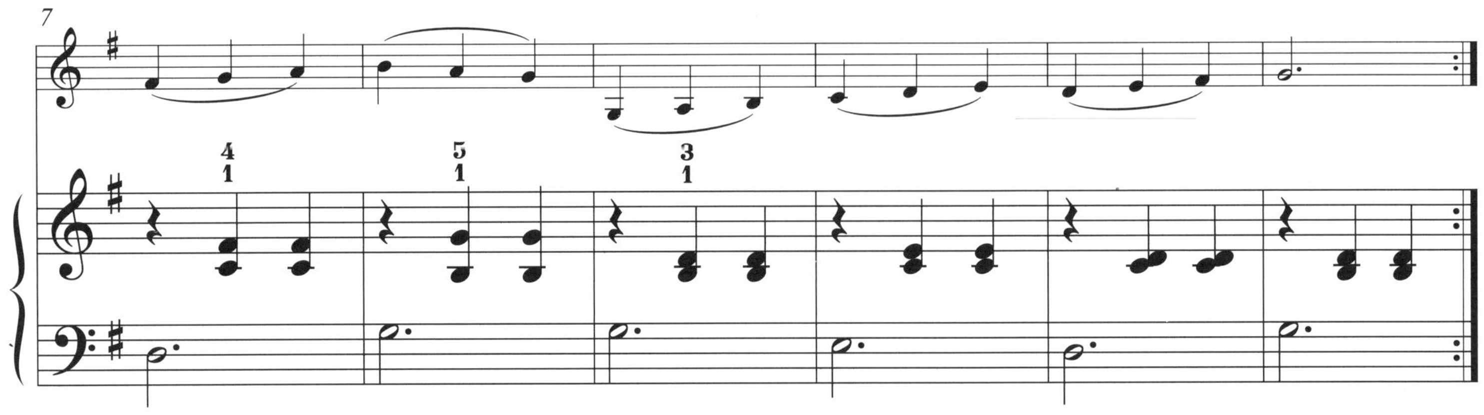

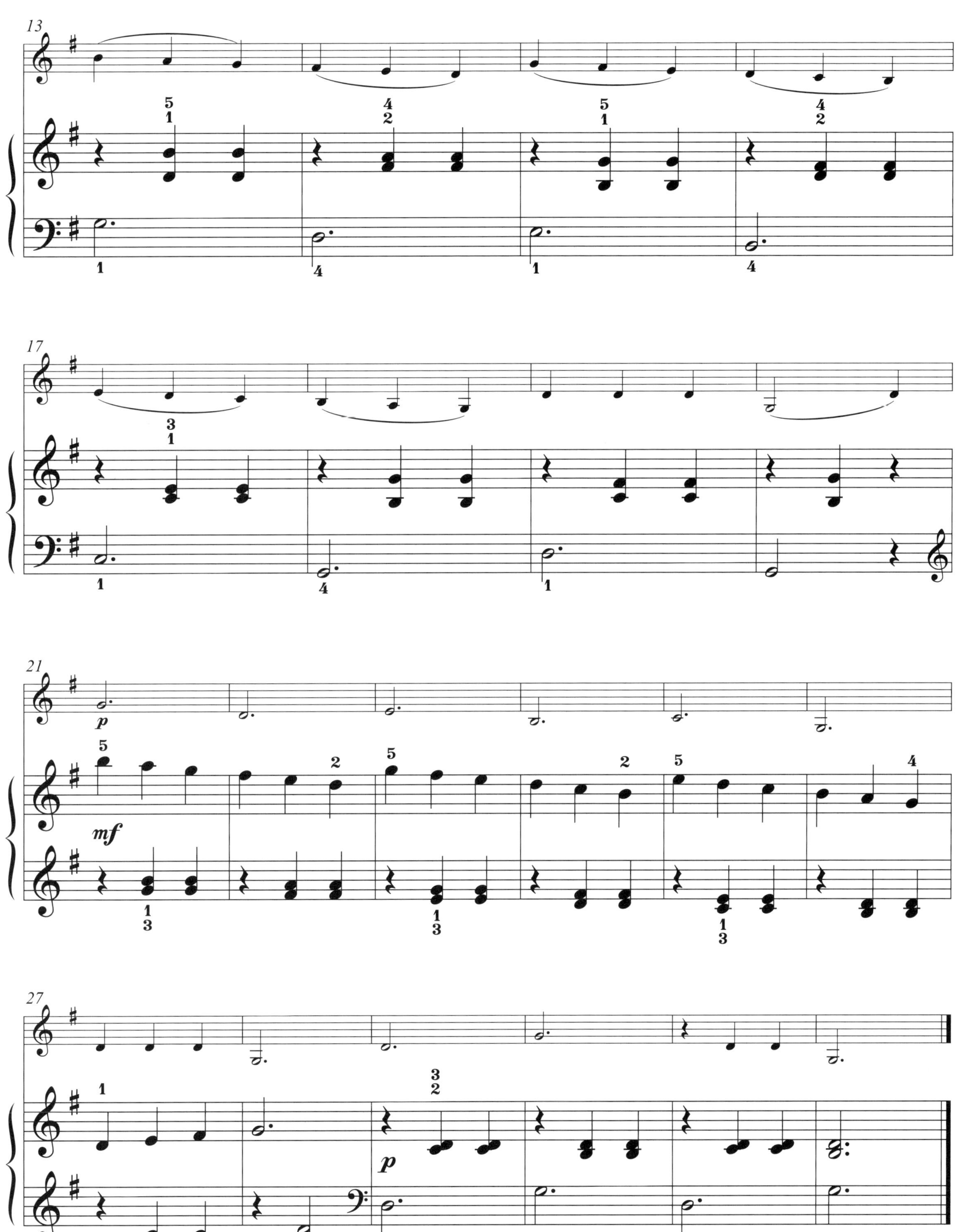
13
17
21
p
mf
27
p

Holterdipolter

Helter-Skelter

Schnell
Quickly

Karin Groß

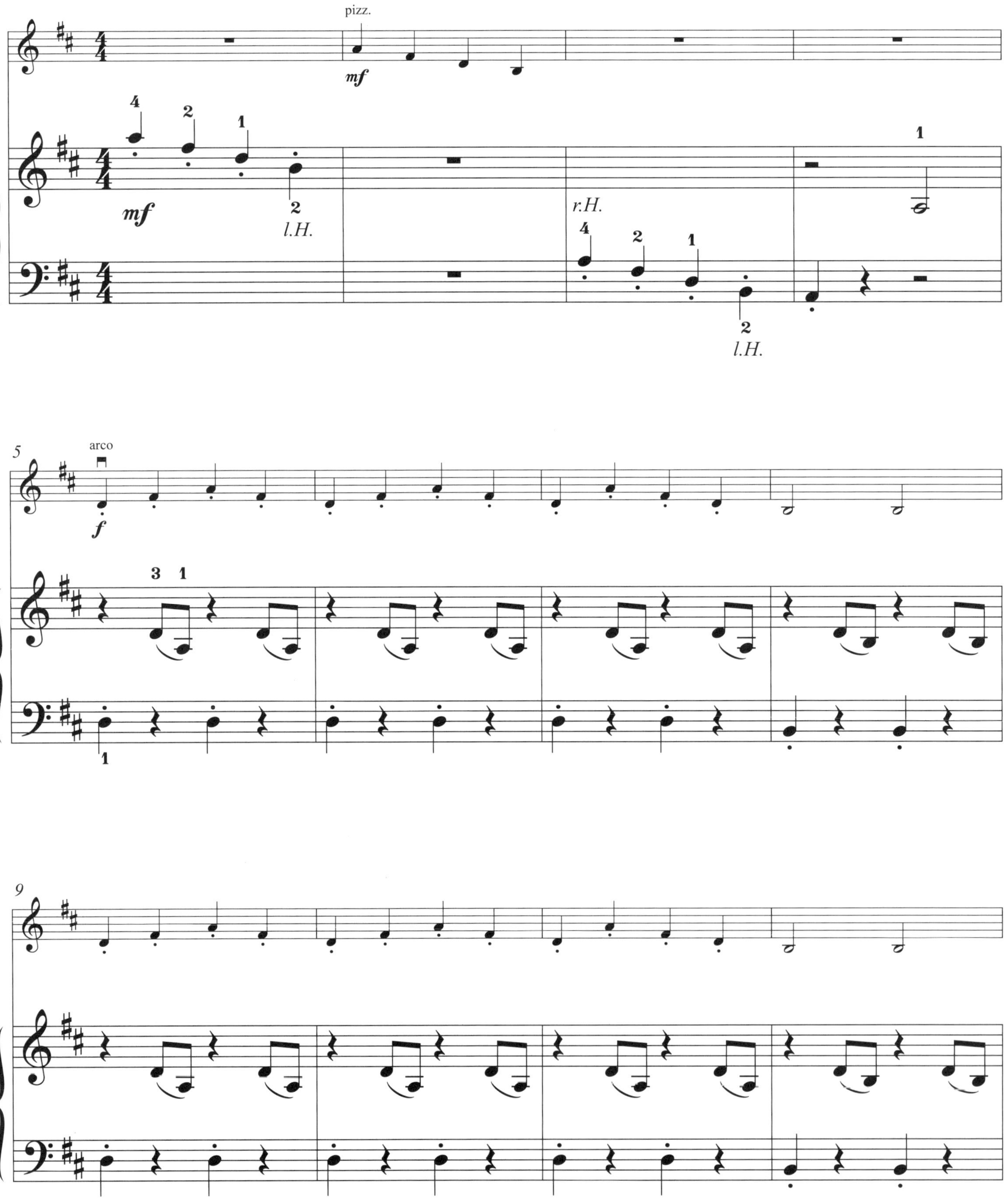

pizz.
mf
4 2 1
mf
2
l.H.
1
r.H.
4 2 1
2
l.H.

5
arco
f
3 1
1

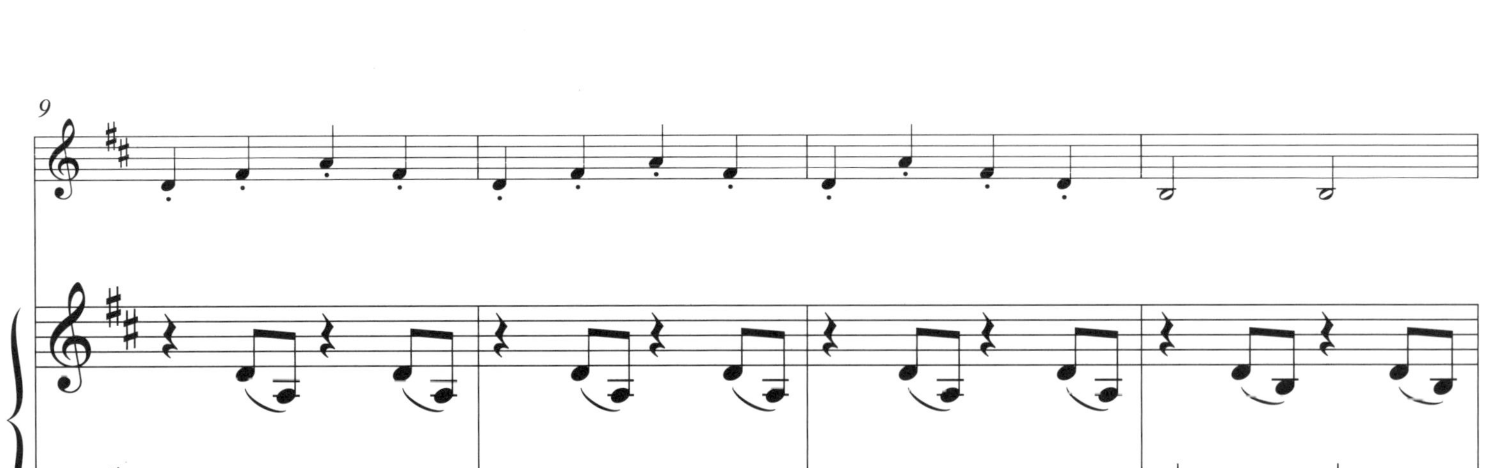

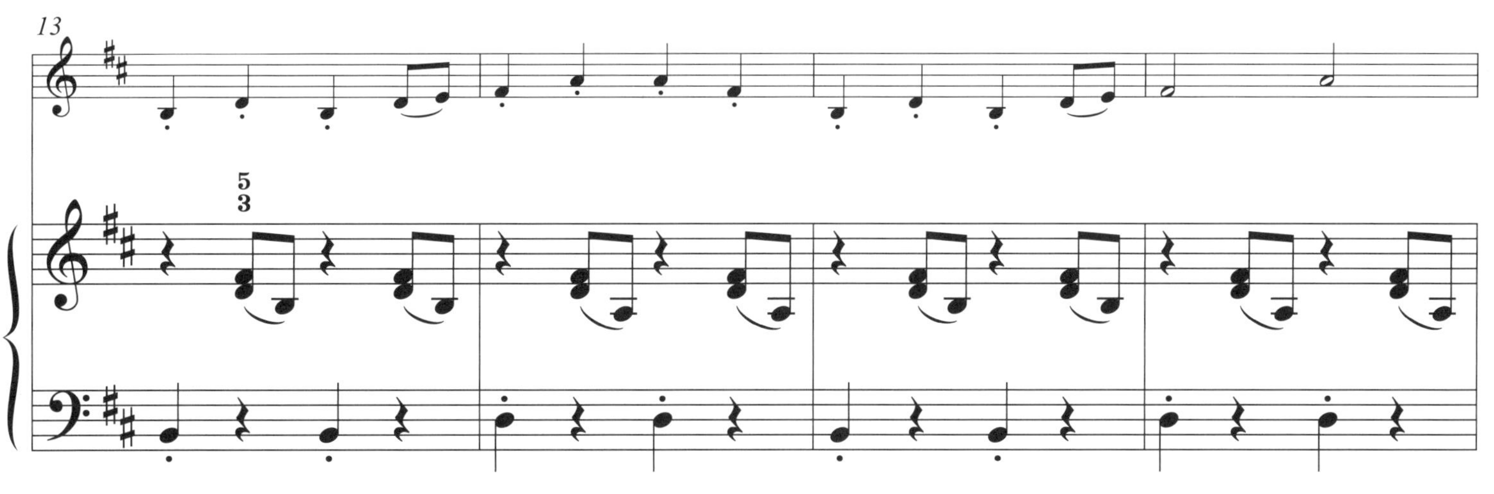
13
5
3

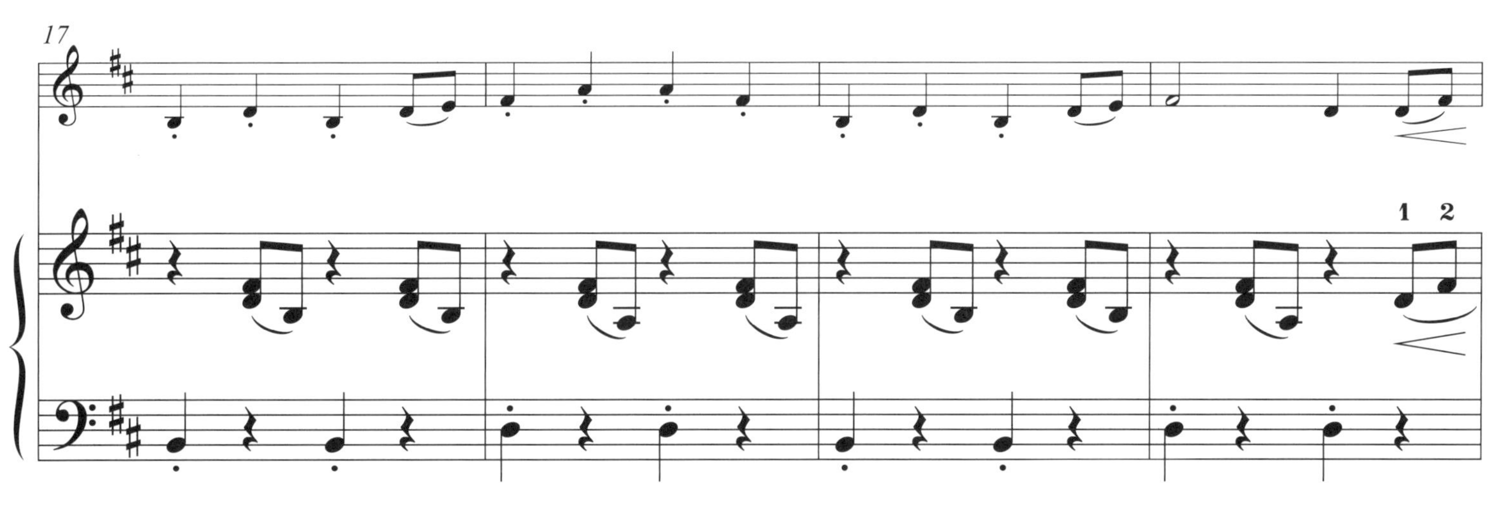
17
1 2

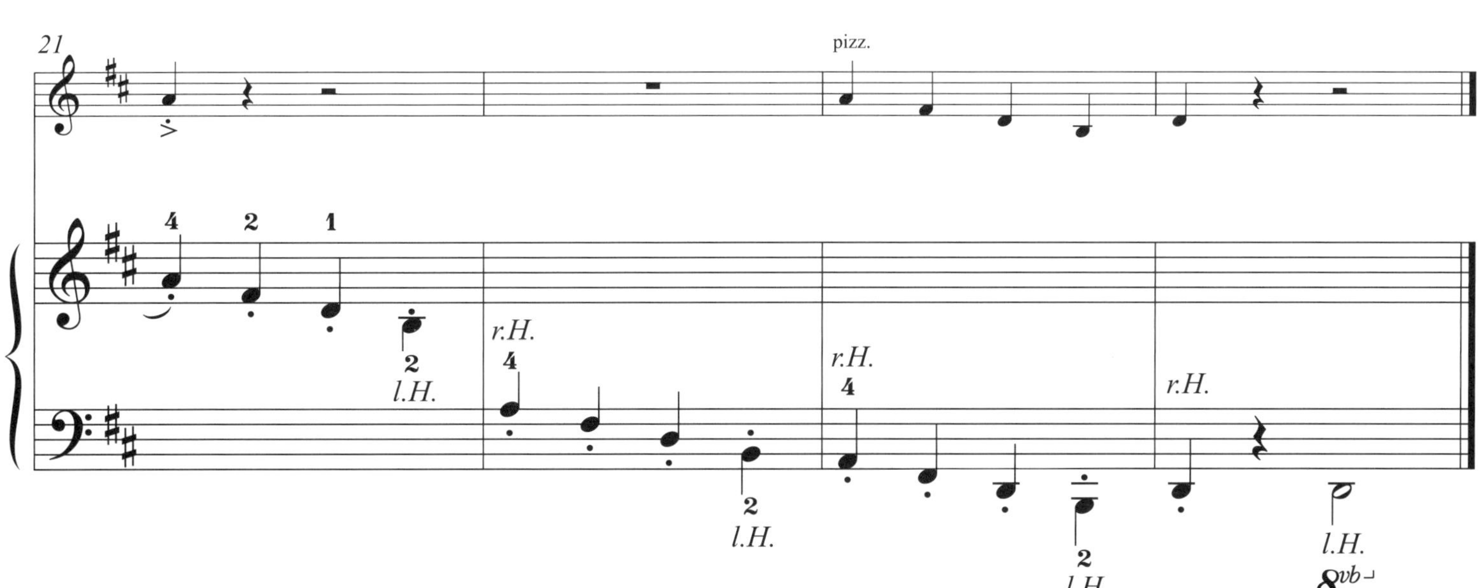
21
pizz.
4 2 1
2
l.H.
r.H.
4
2
l.H.
r.H.
4
2
l.H.
r.H.
l.H.
8vb

Im Bambushain

In The Bamboo Grove

Karin Groß

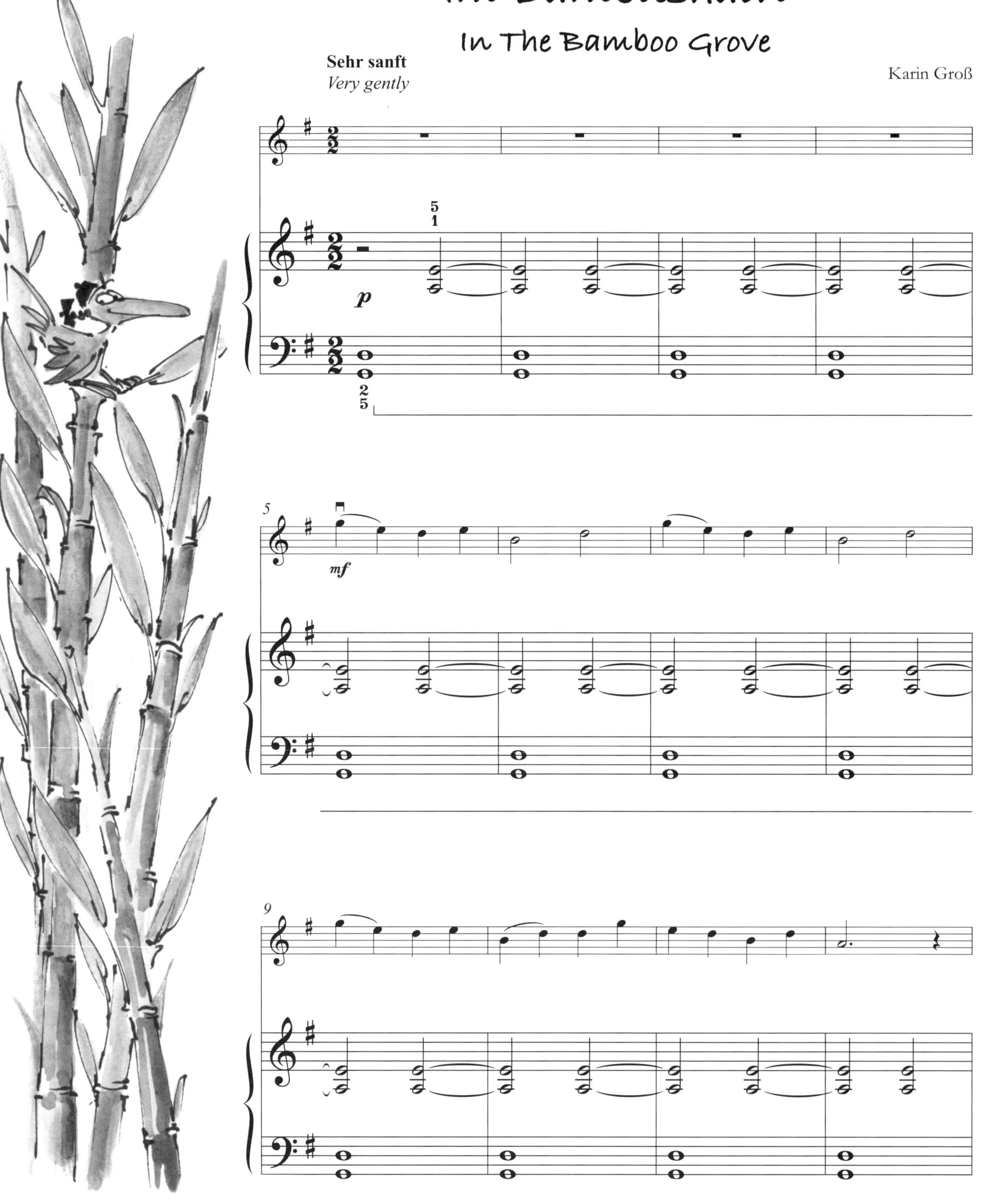

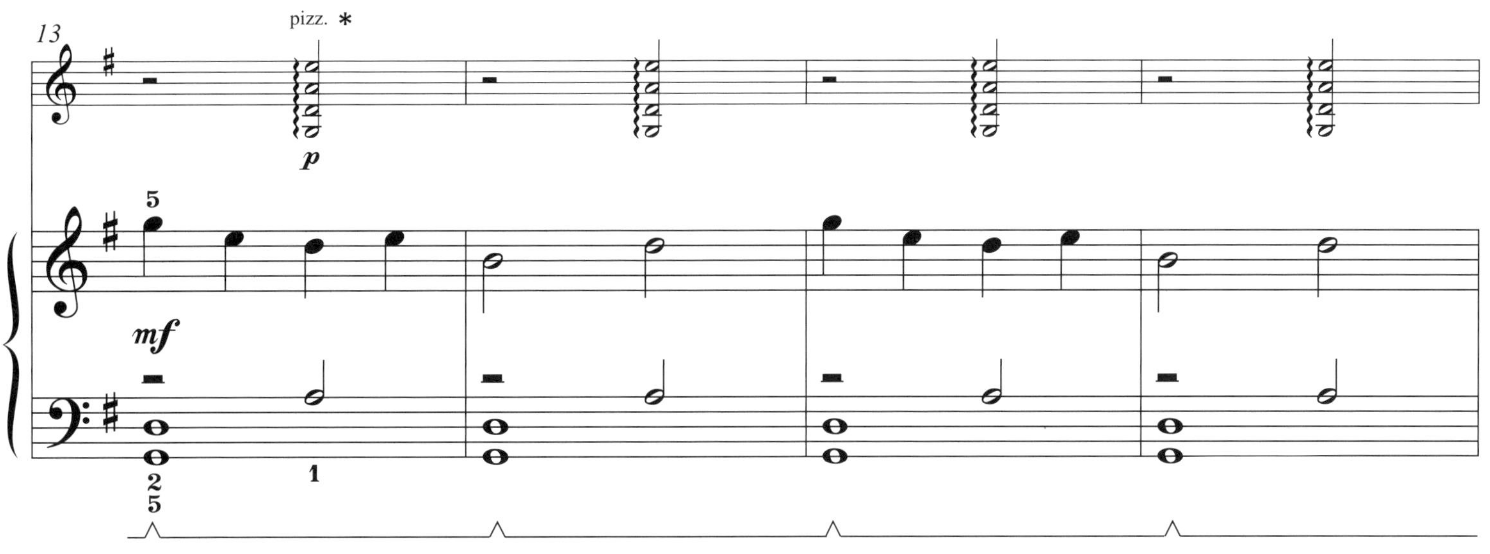

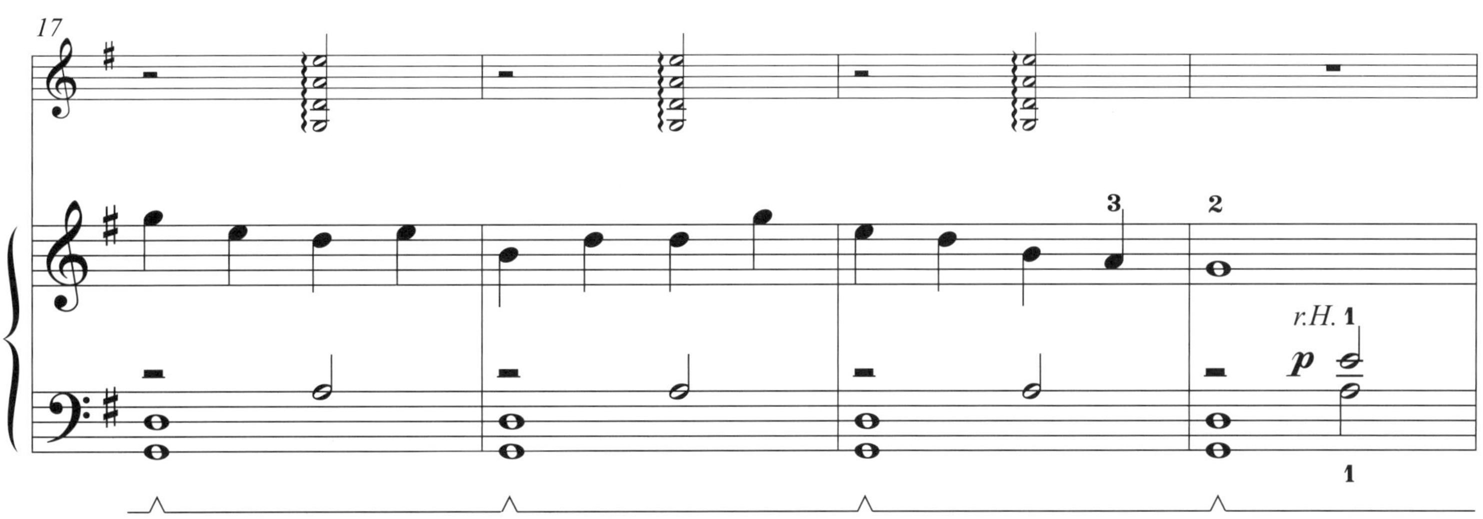

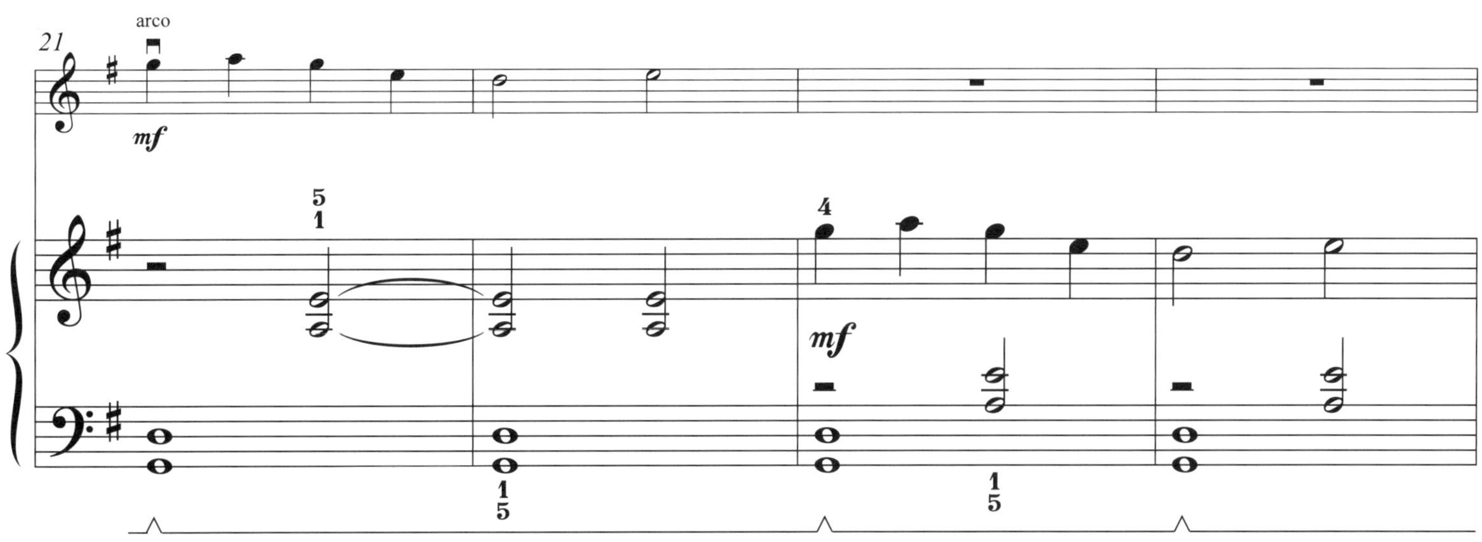

* Weiche, langsame Arpeggien / *Gentle, slow arpeggios*

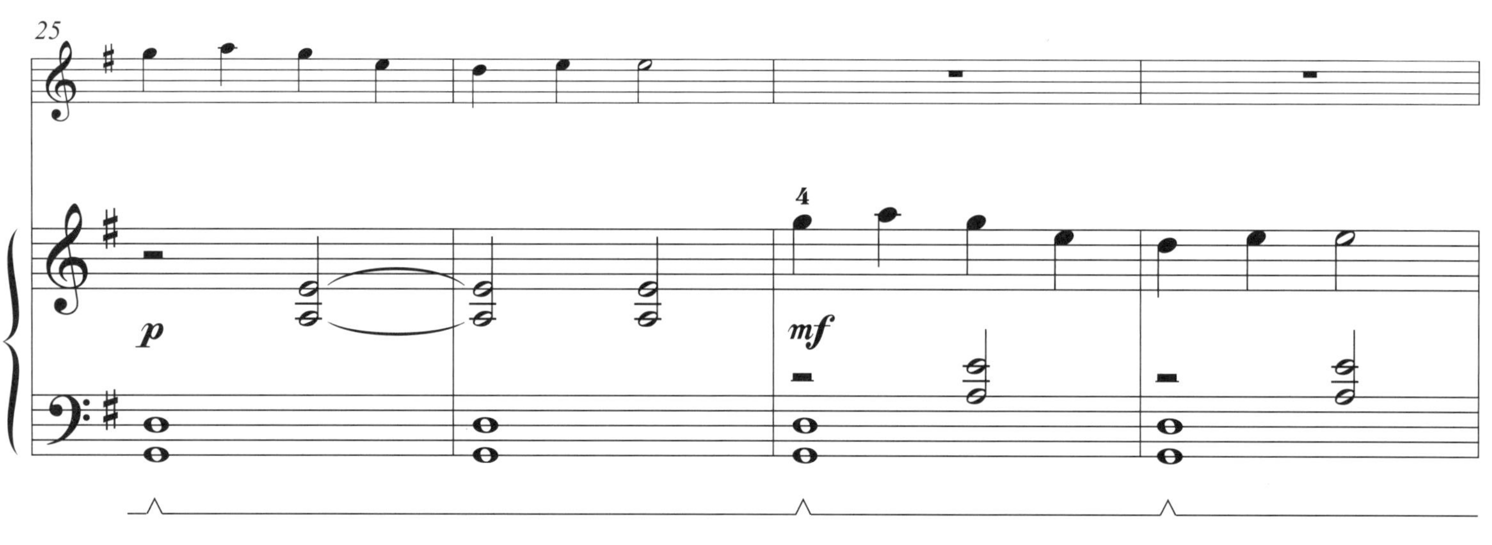
25
4
p
mf

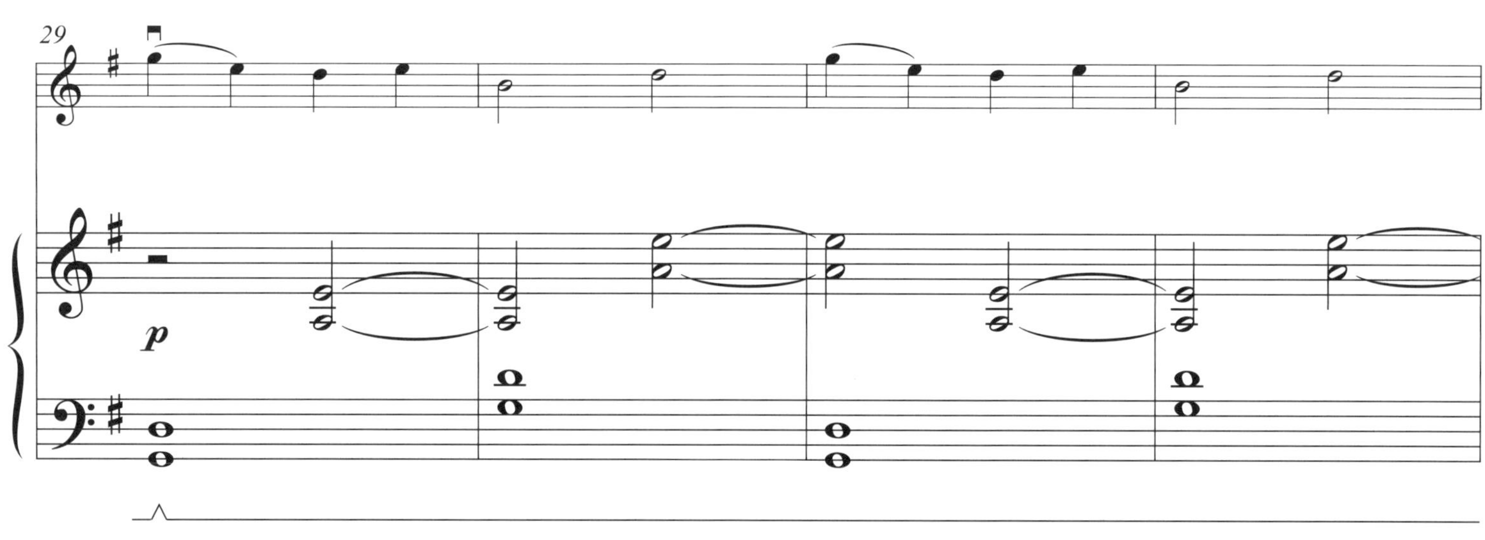
29
p

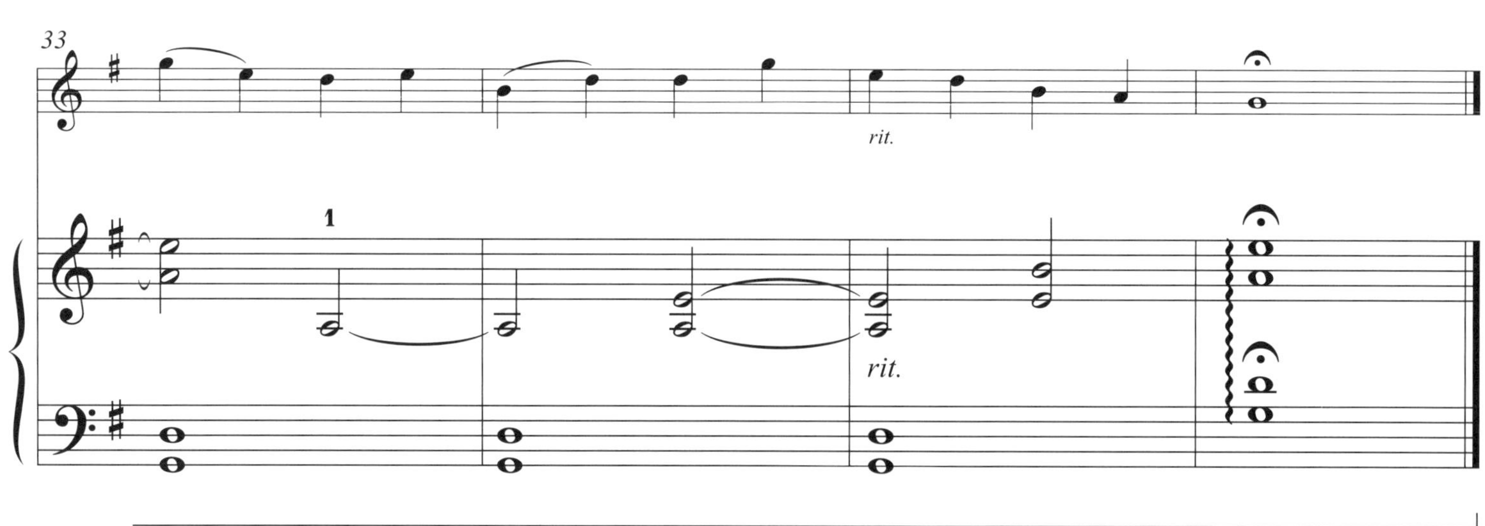
33
1
rit.
rit.

Lullaby

Behaglich
Contentedly

Karin Groß

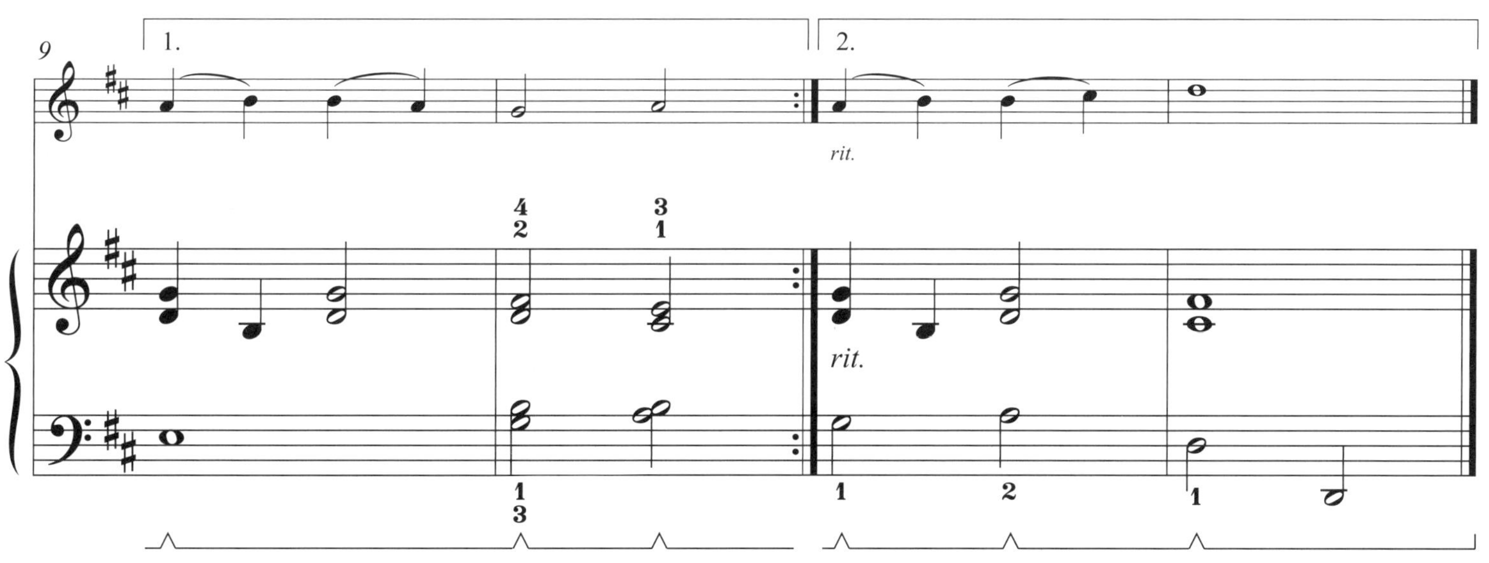

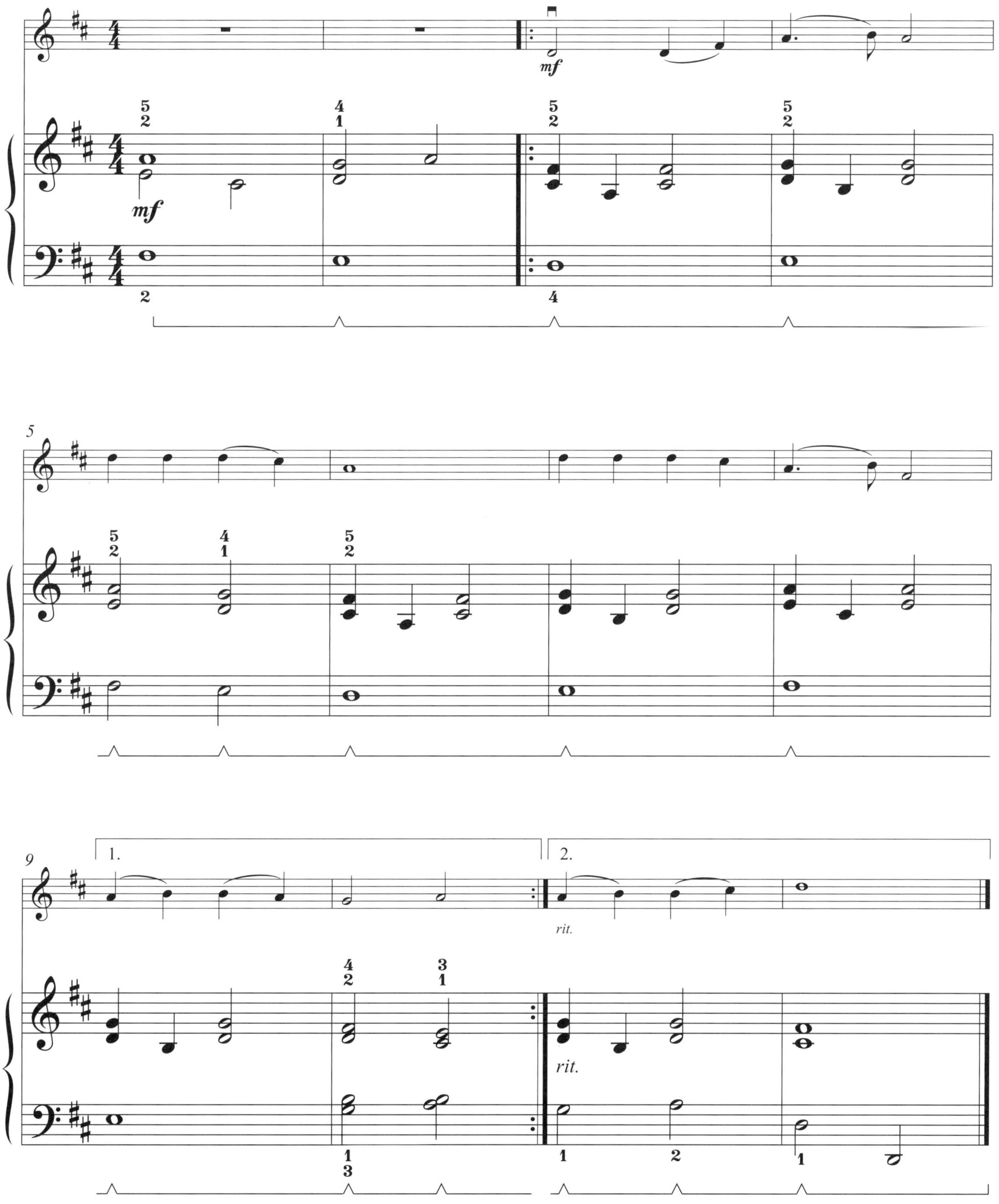

Familie Frosch

The Frog Family

Übermütig
Boisterously

Karin Groß

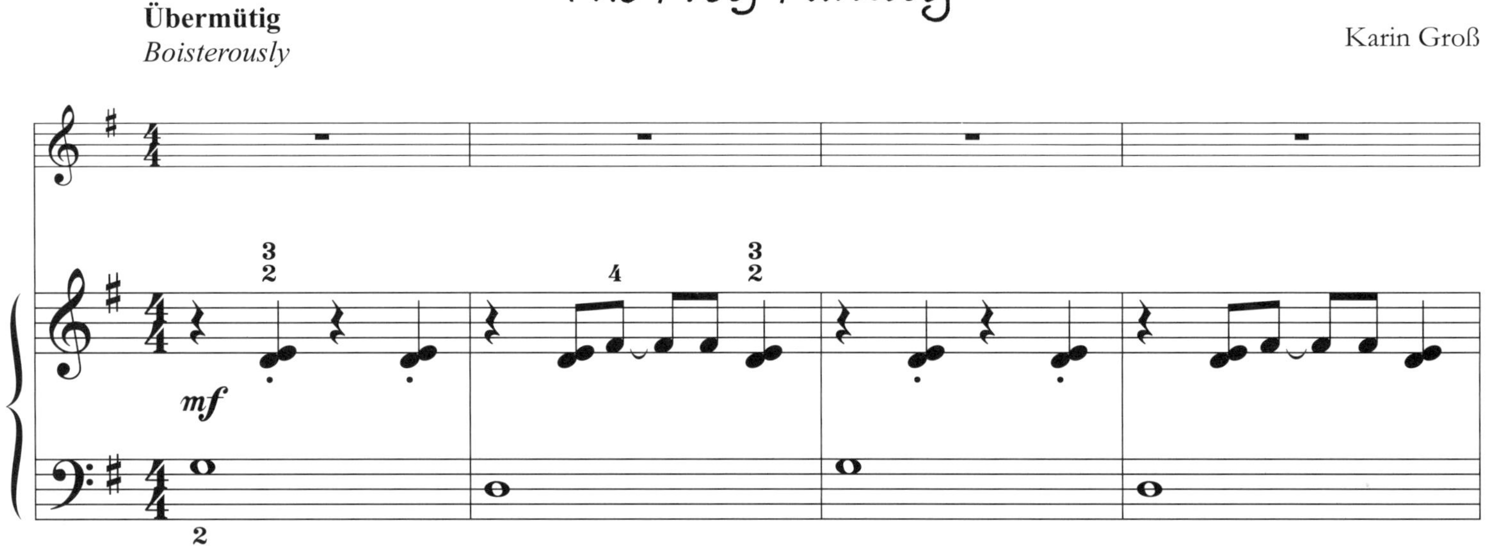

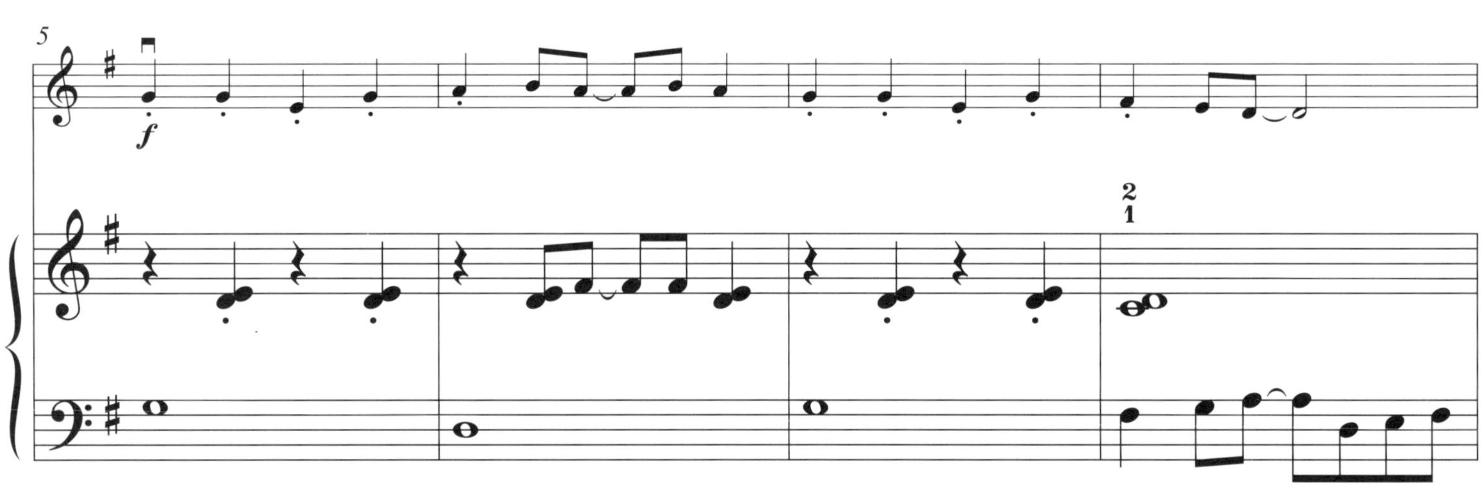

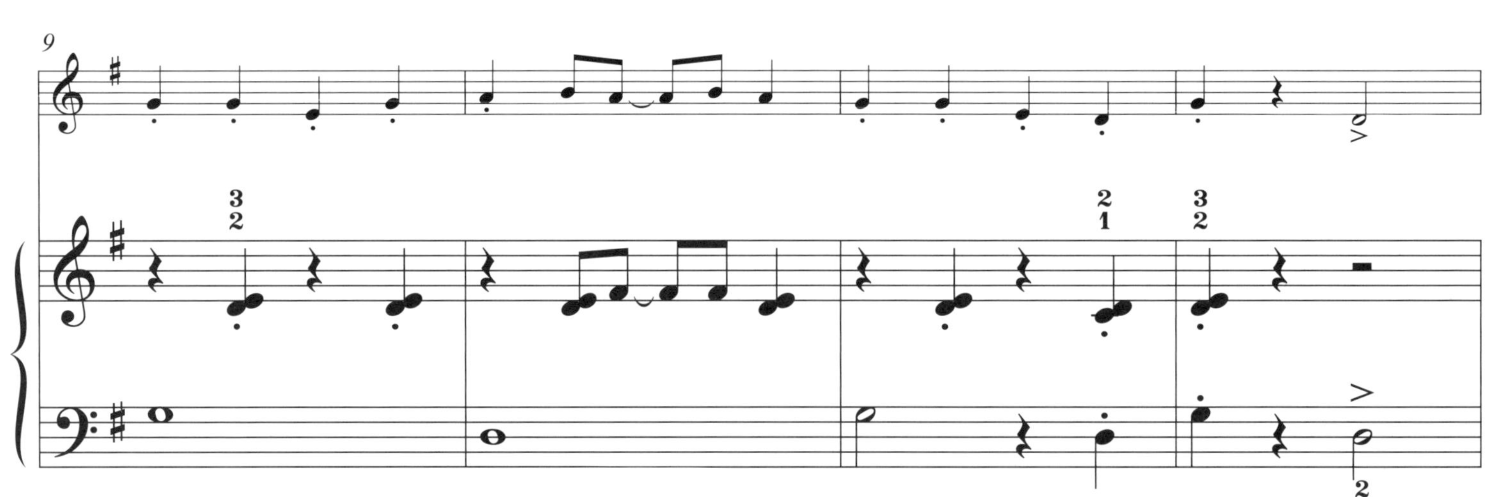

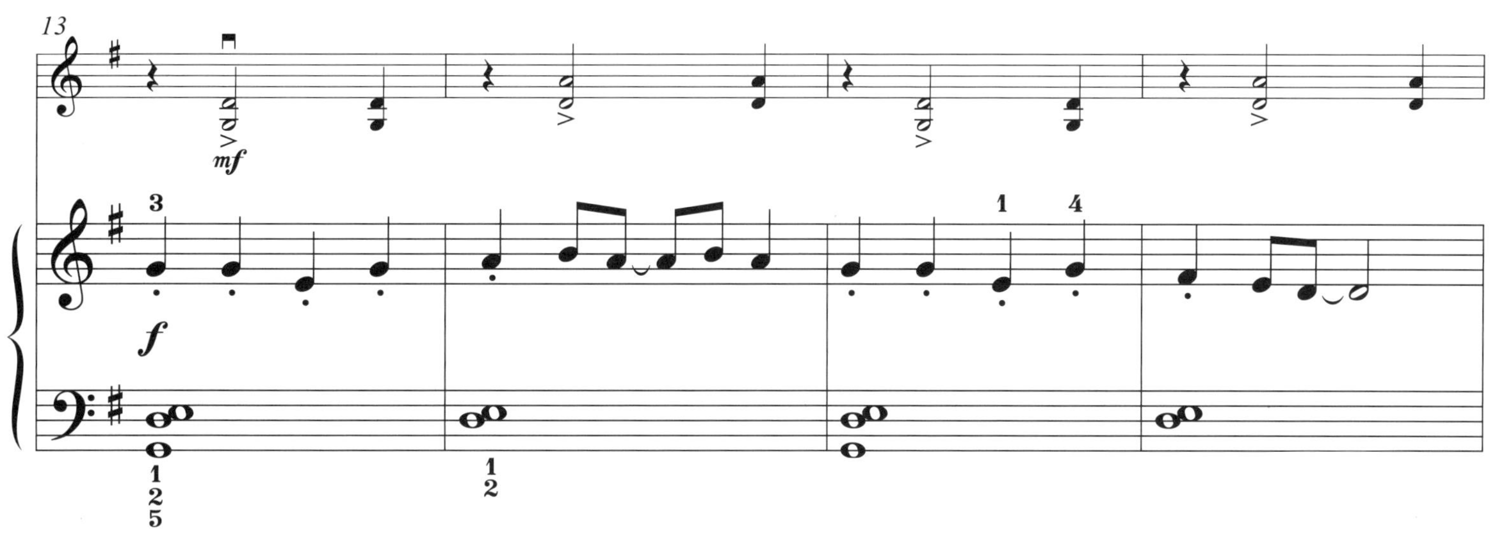
13
mf
f
3
1
4
1
2
5
1
2

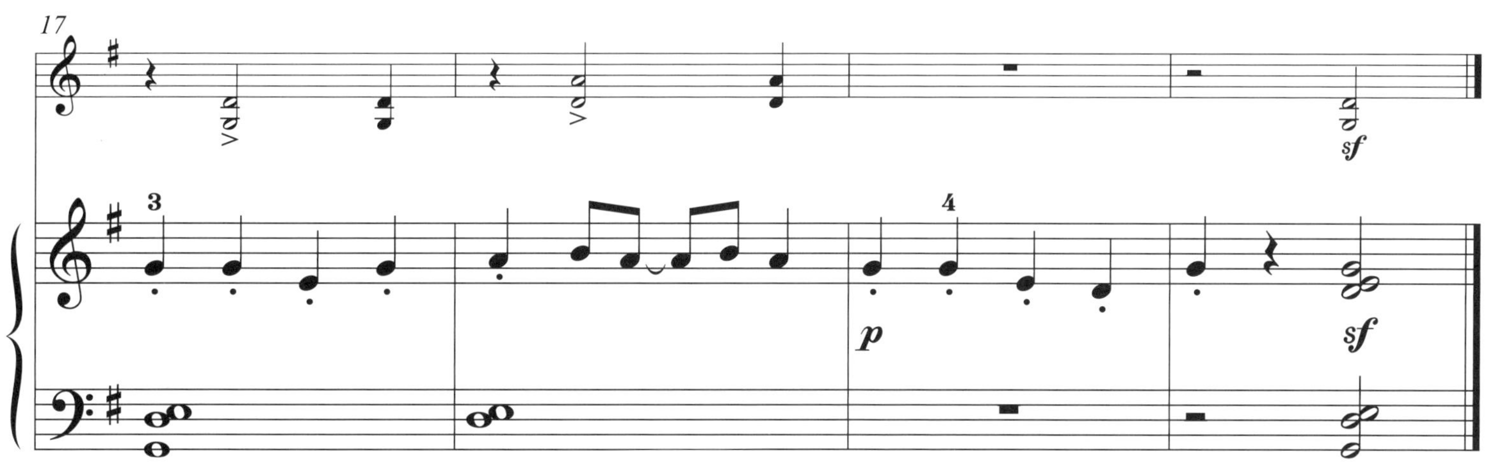
17
sf
3
4
p
sf

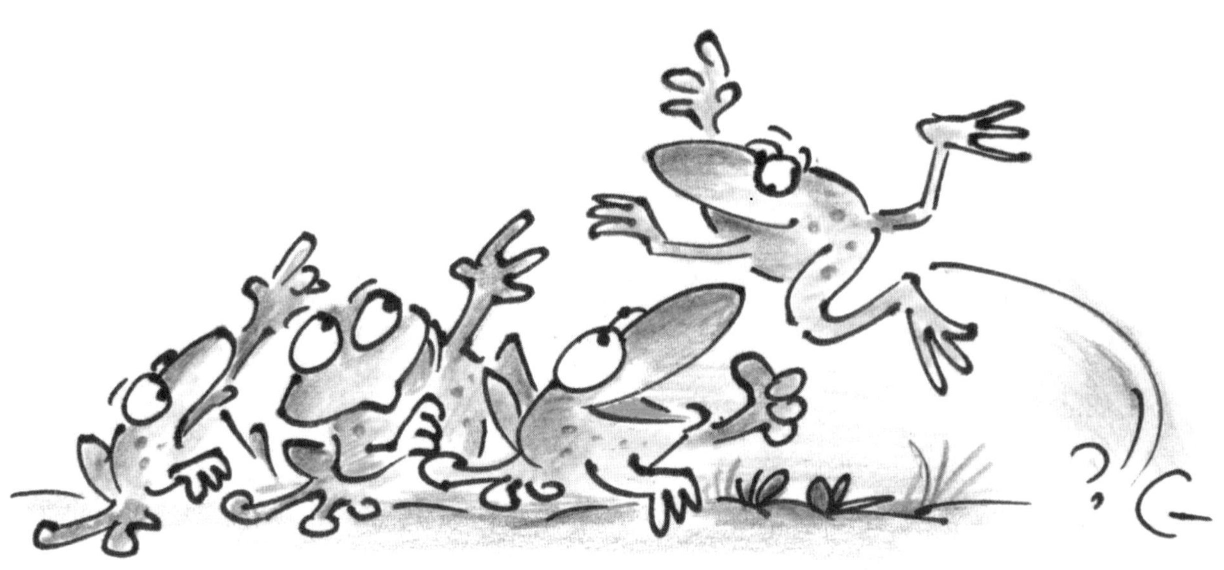

Fröhlich gepfiffen

Merrily Whistled

Karin Groß

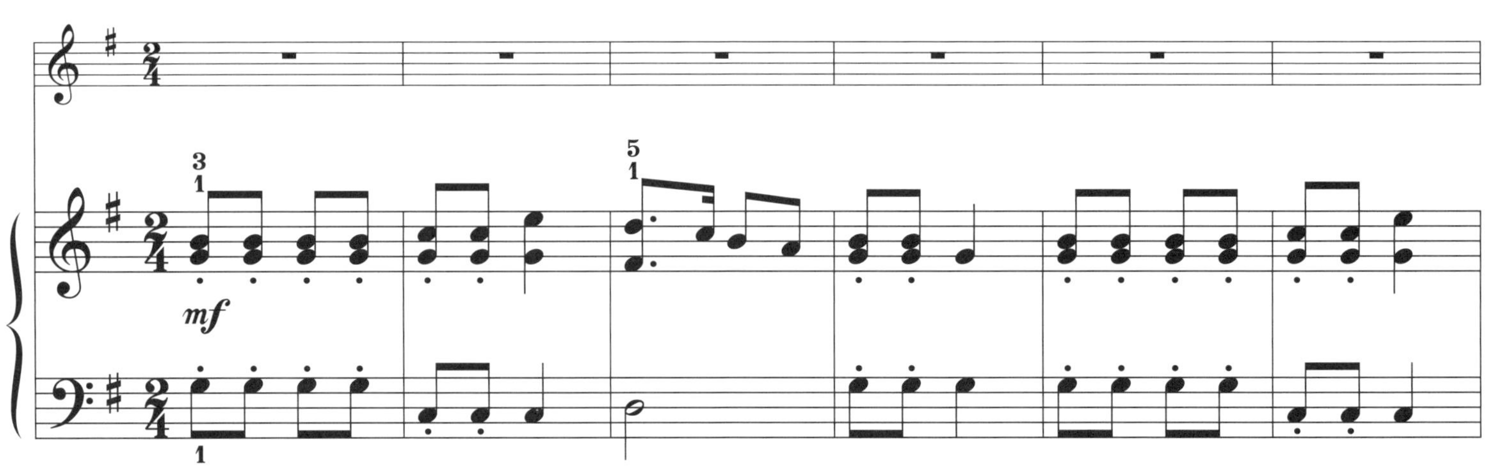

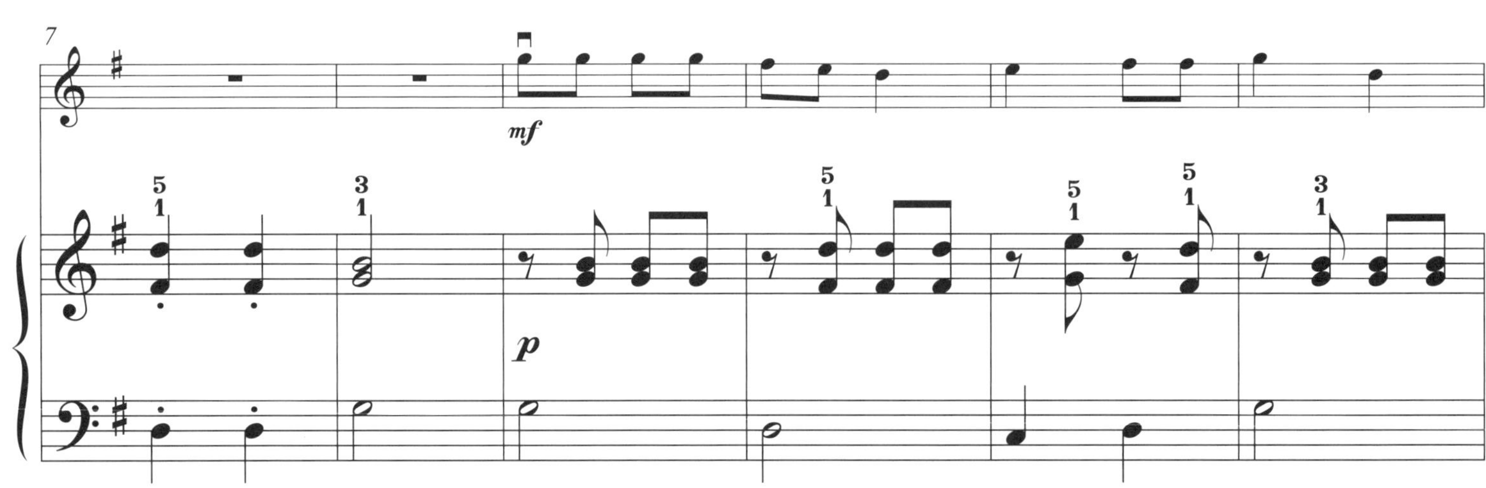

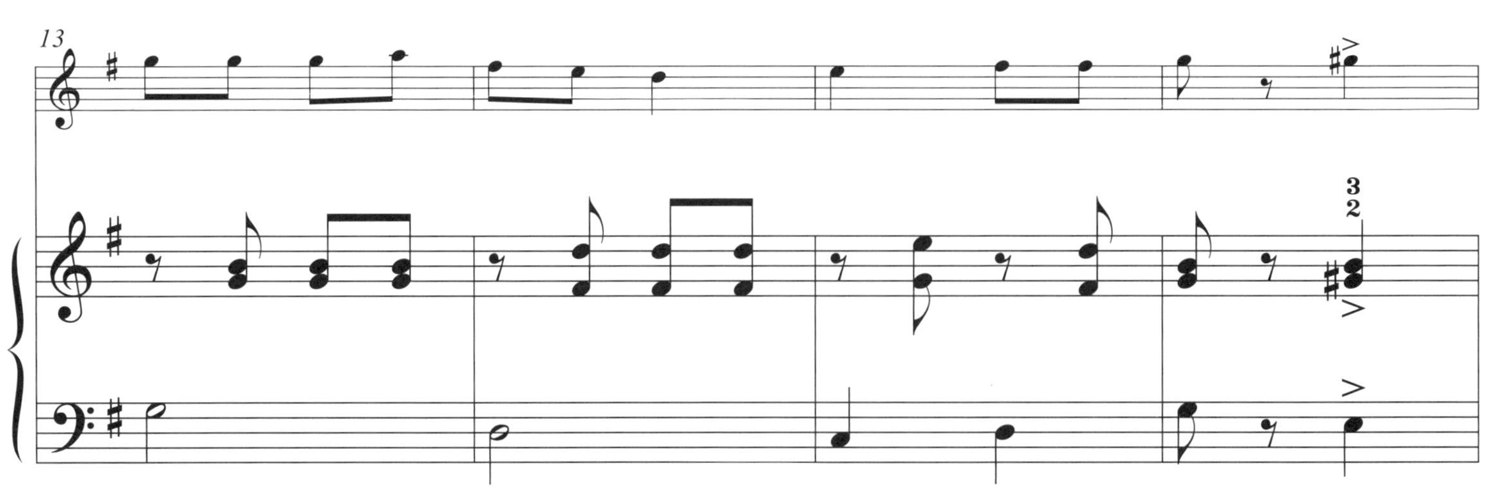

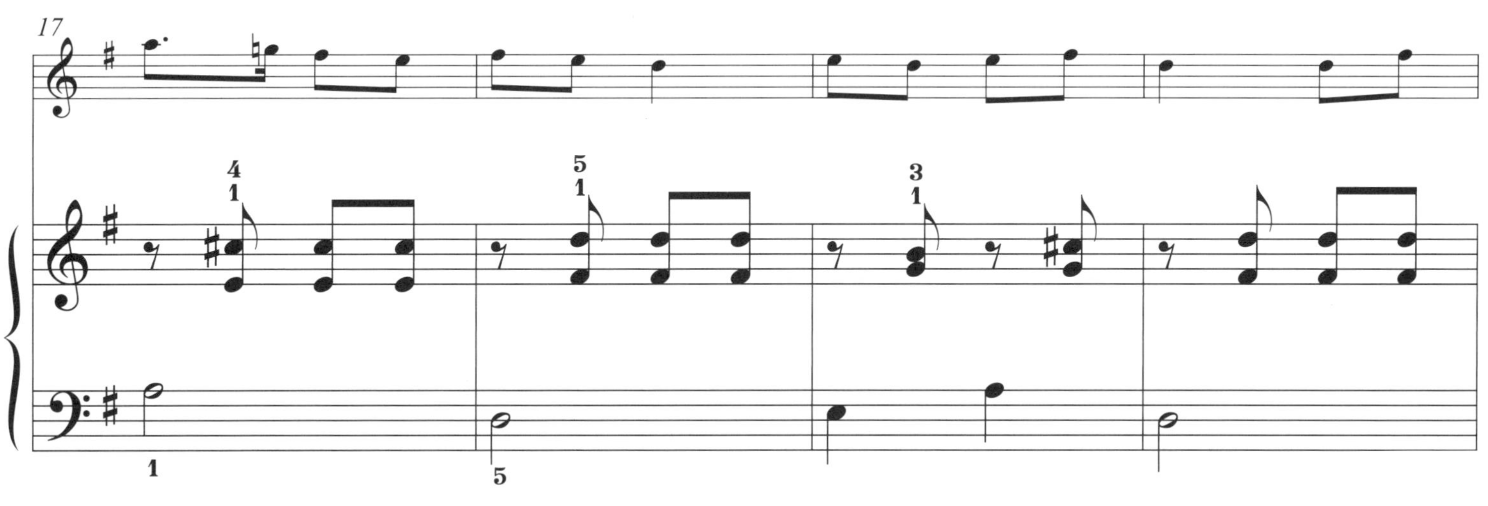
17
4
1
5
1
3
1
1
5

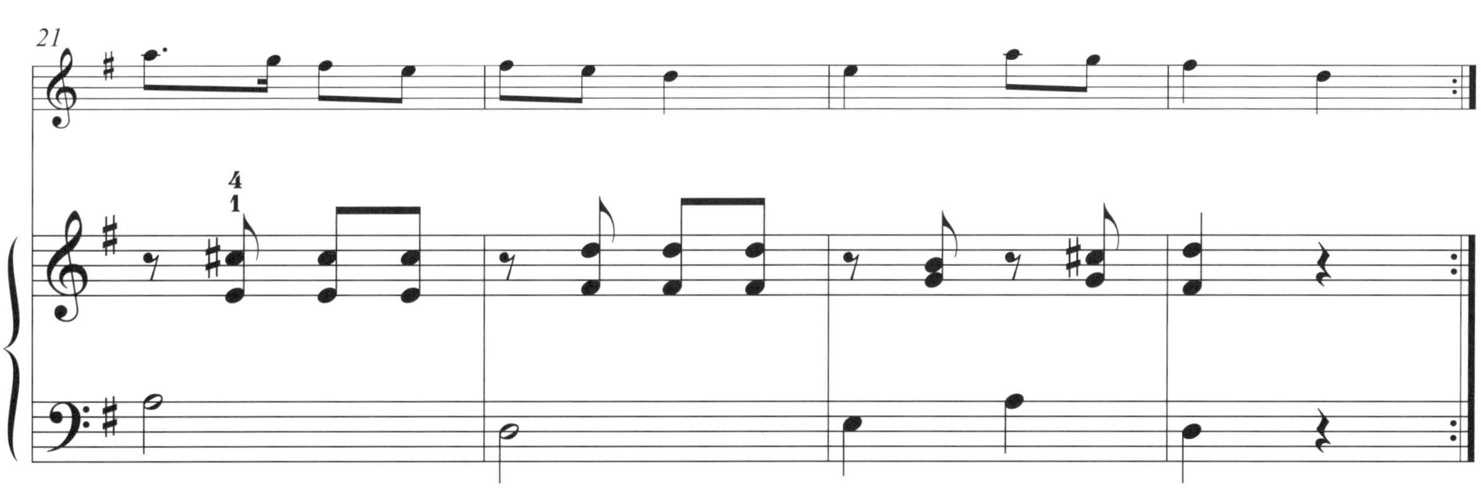
21
4
1

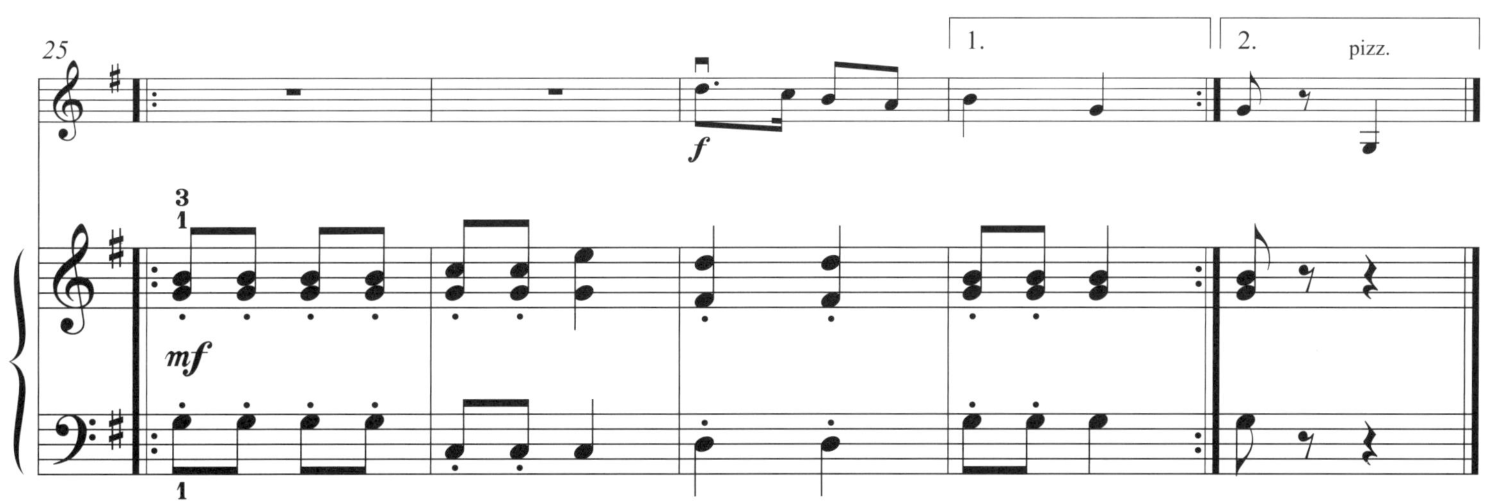
25
1.
2.
pizz.
f
3
1
mf
1

Der Gondoliere

The Gondolier

Elegant
Elegantly

Karin Groß

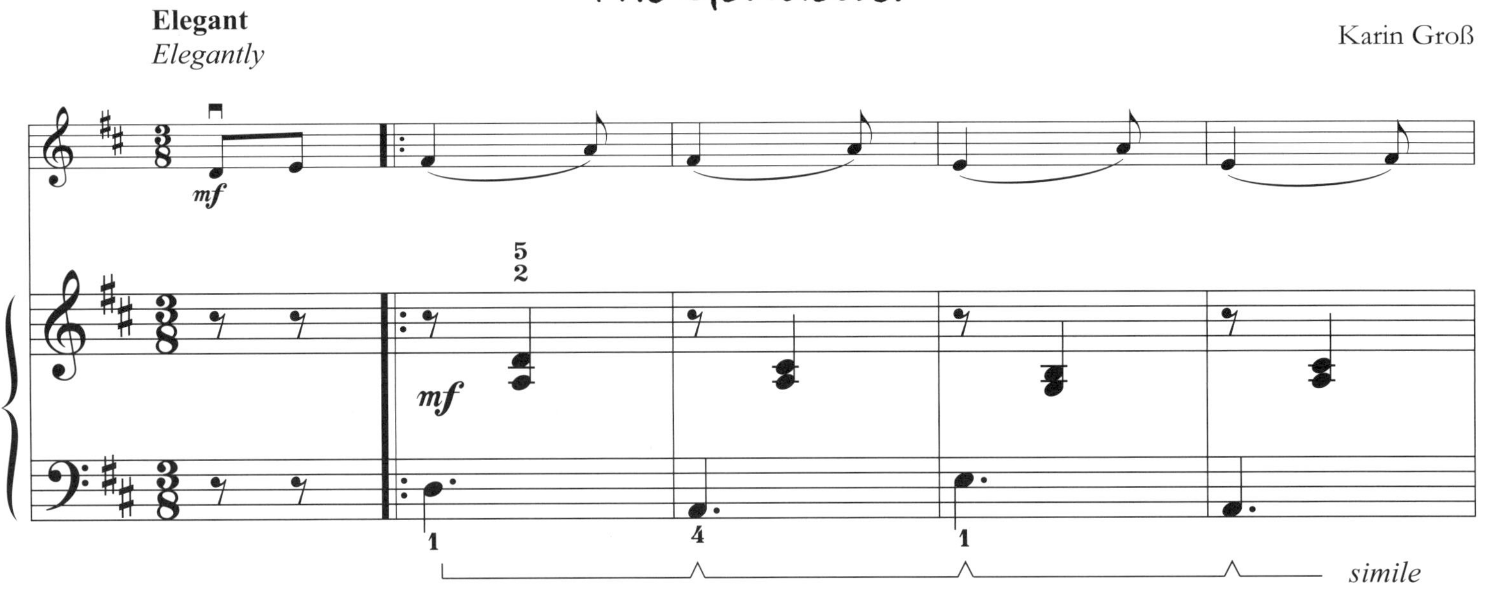

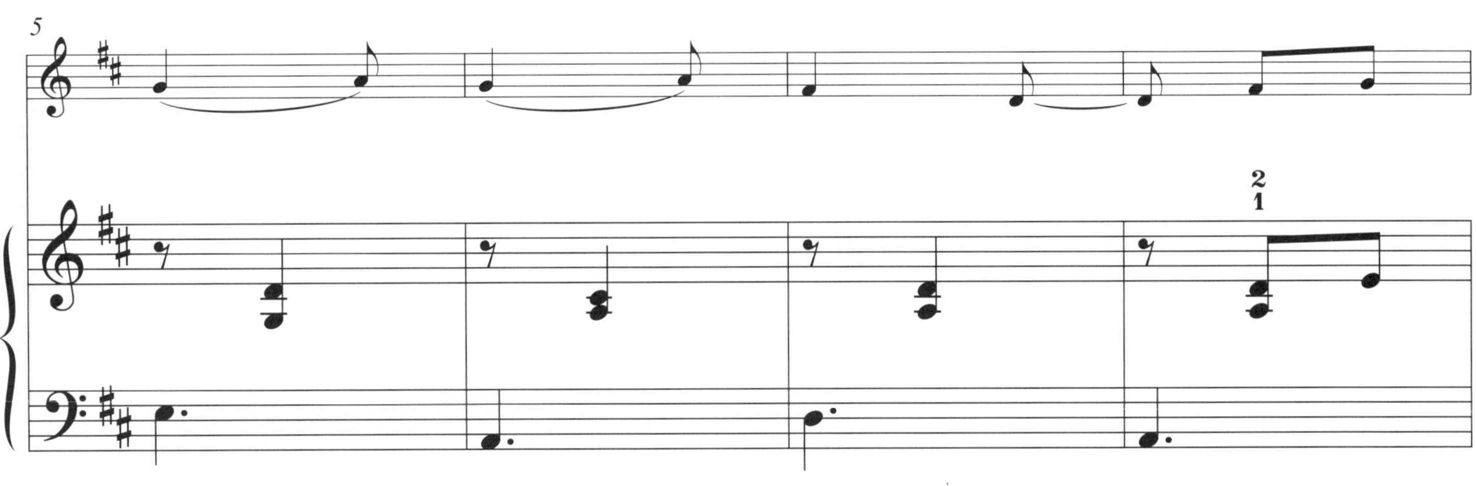

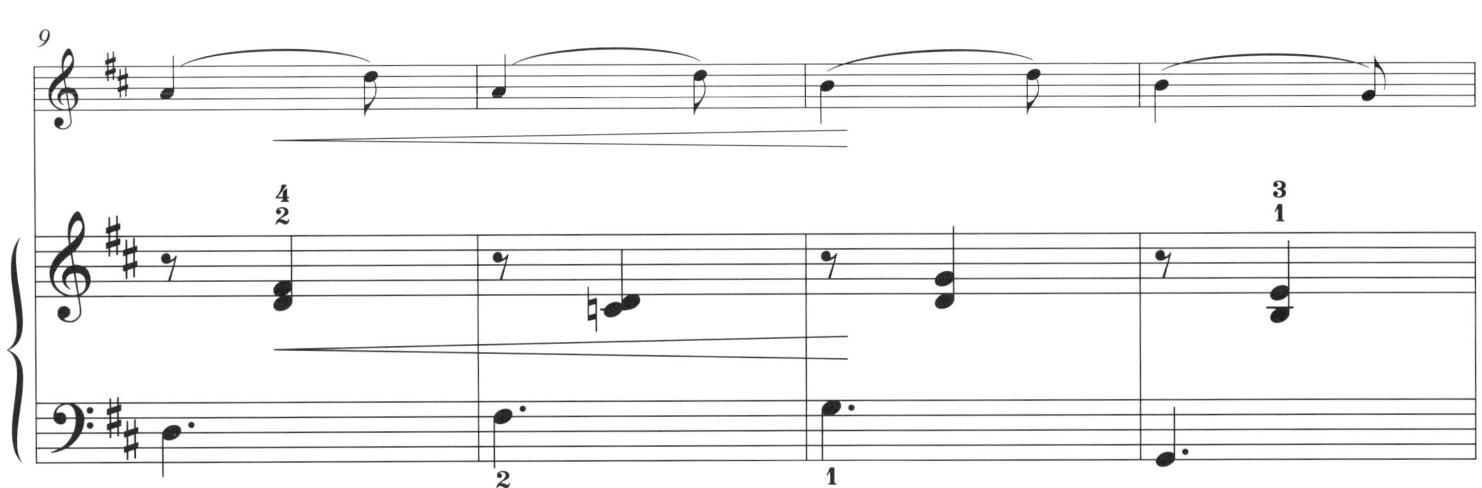

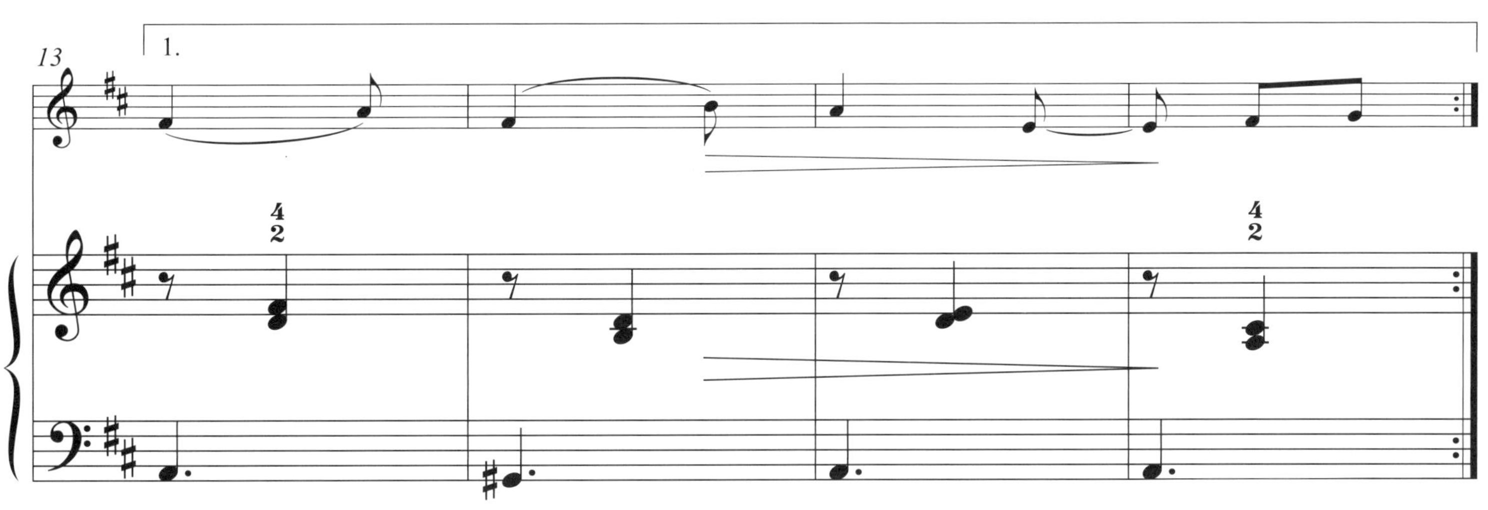

17
2.
4
2
rit.
4
1
rit.

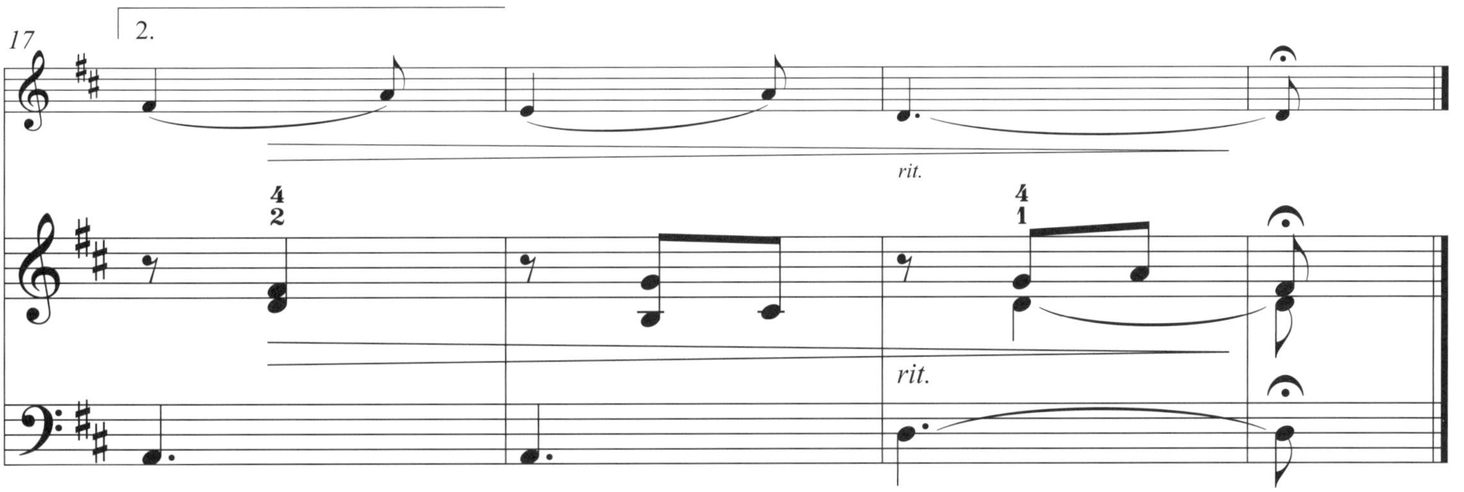

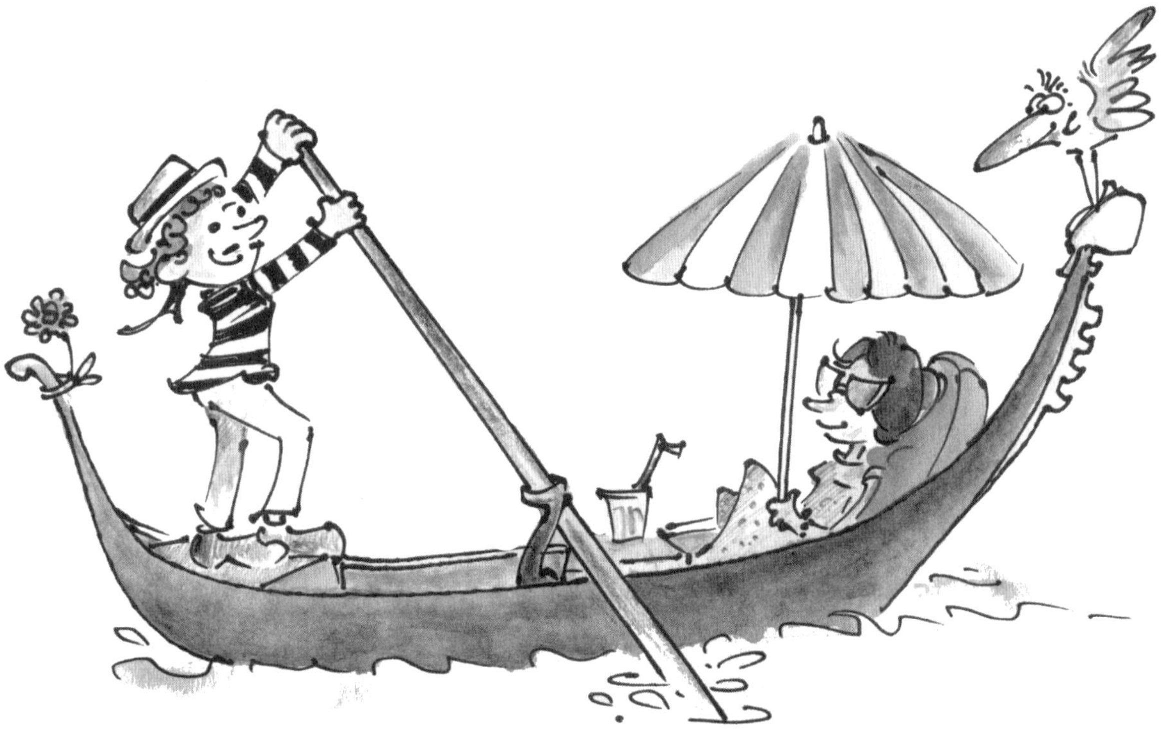

Seeräuber

Pirates

Energisch
Energetically

Karin Groß

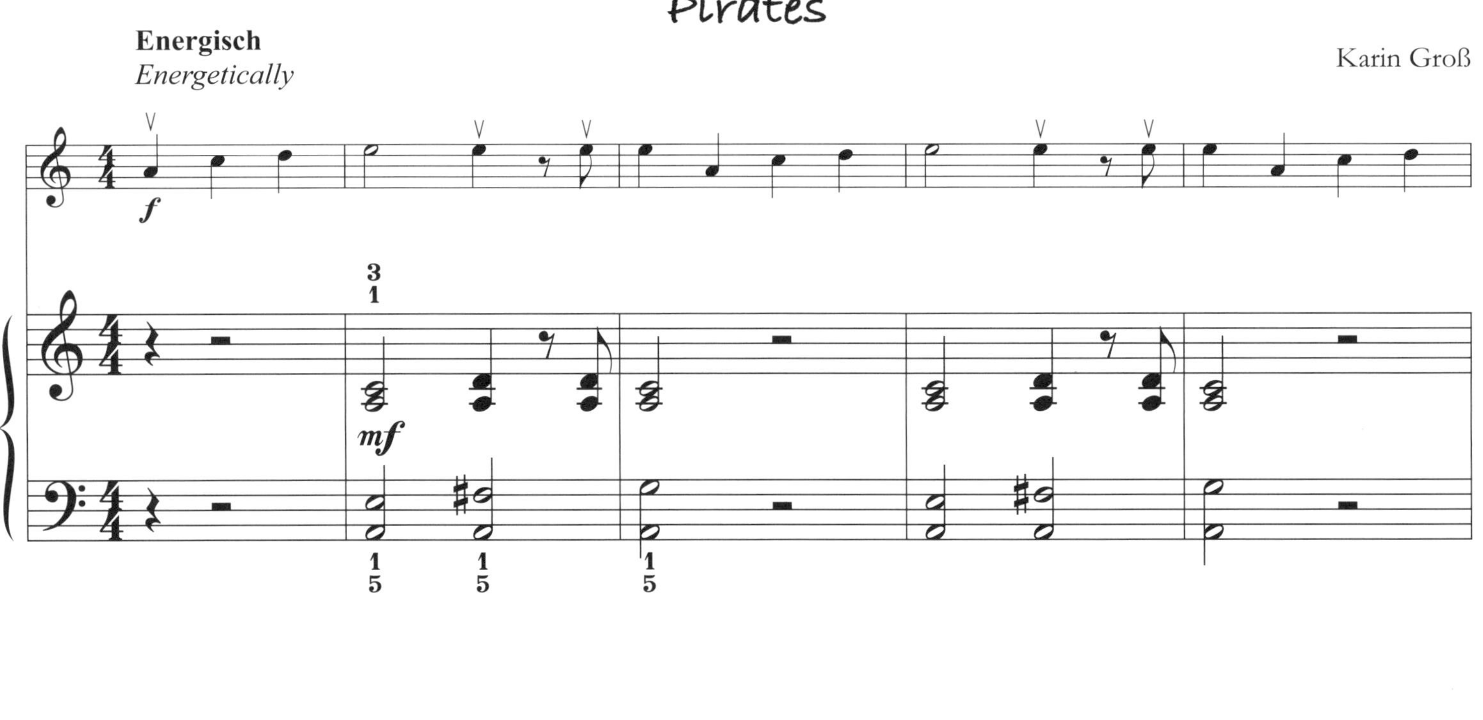

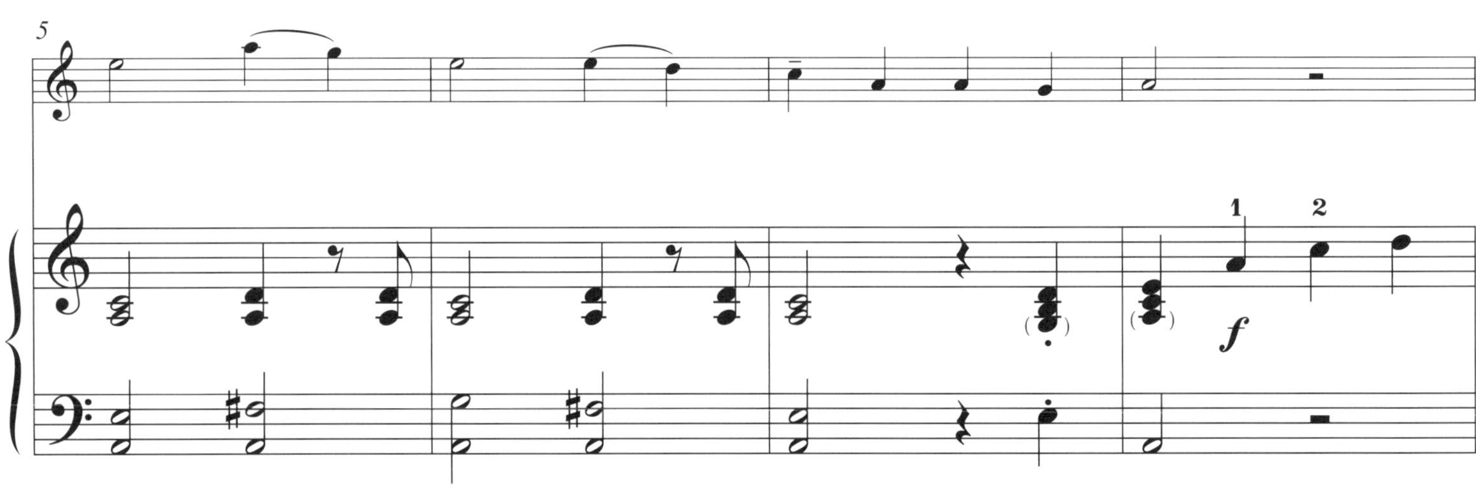

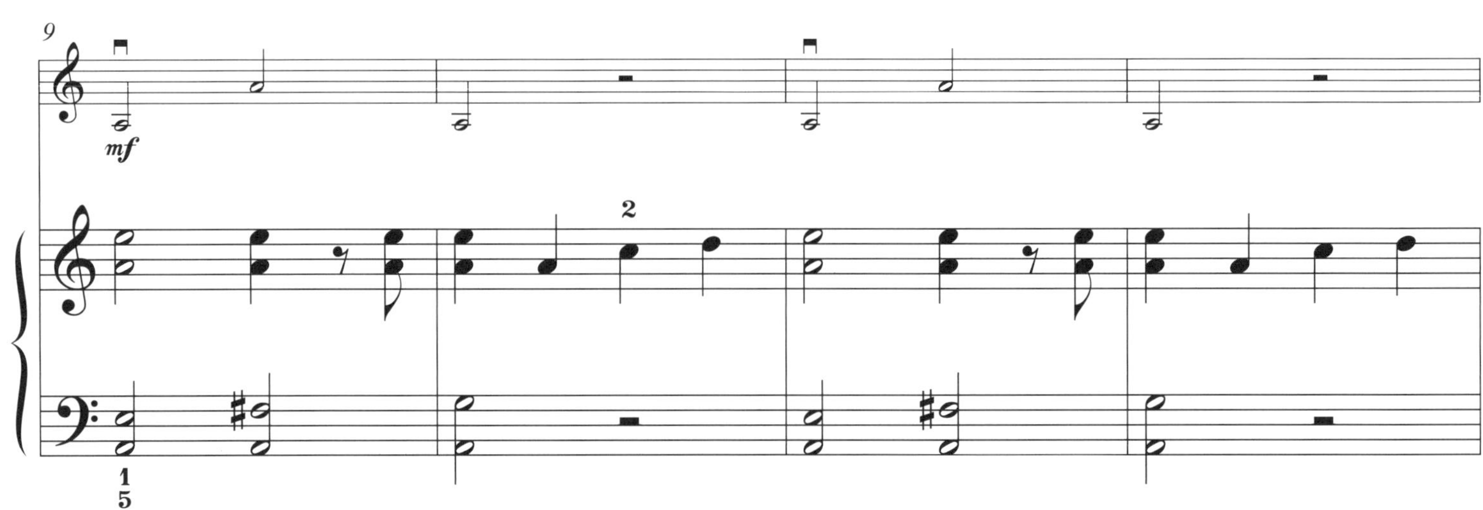

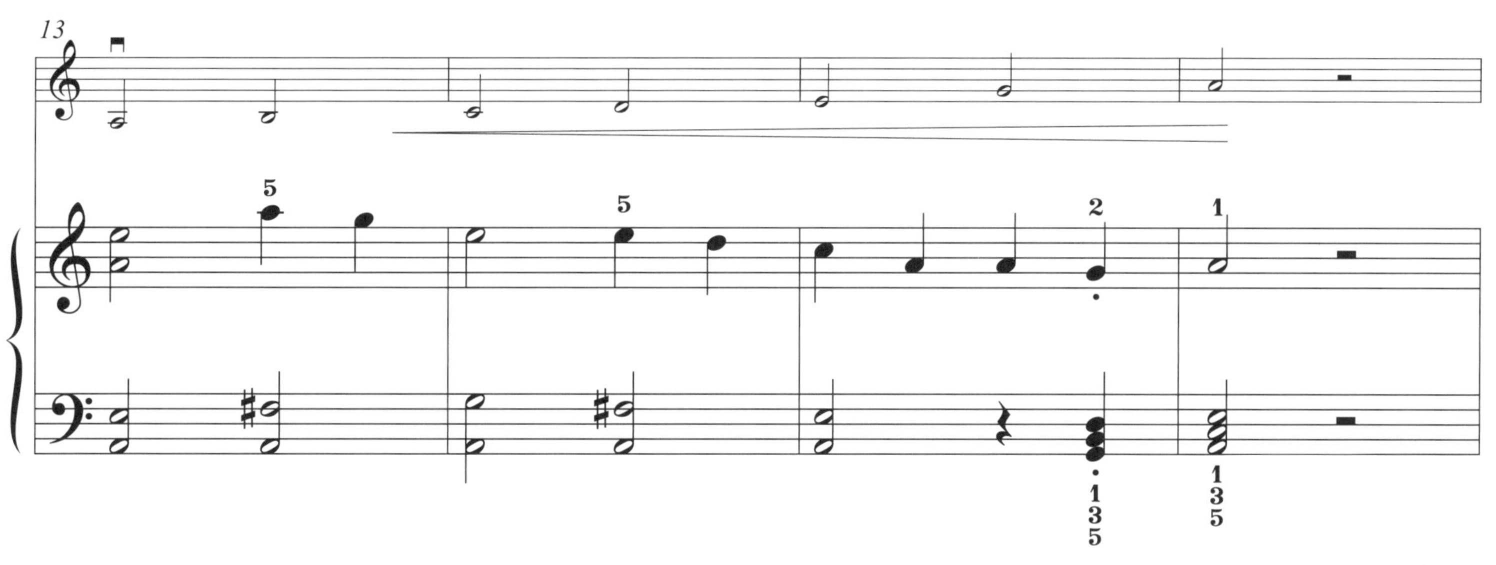
13

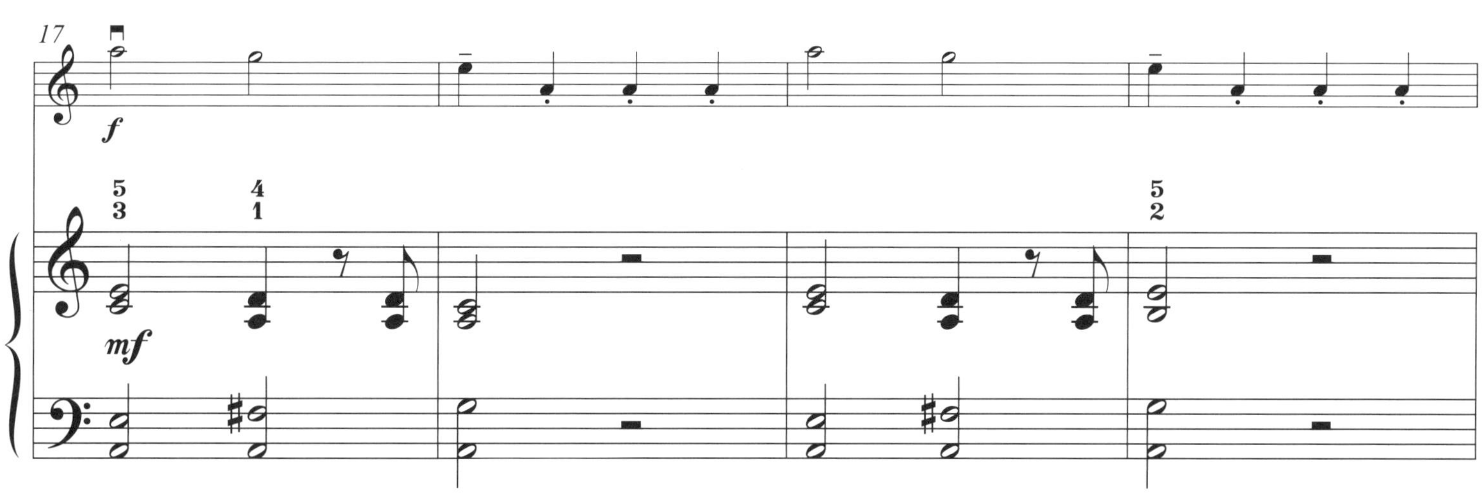
17
f
mf

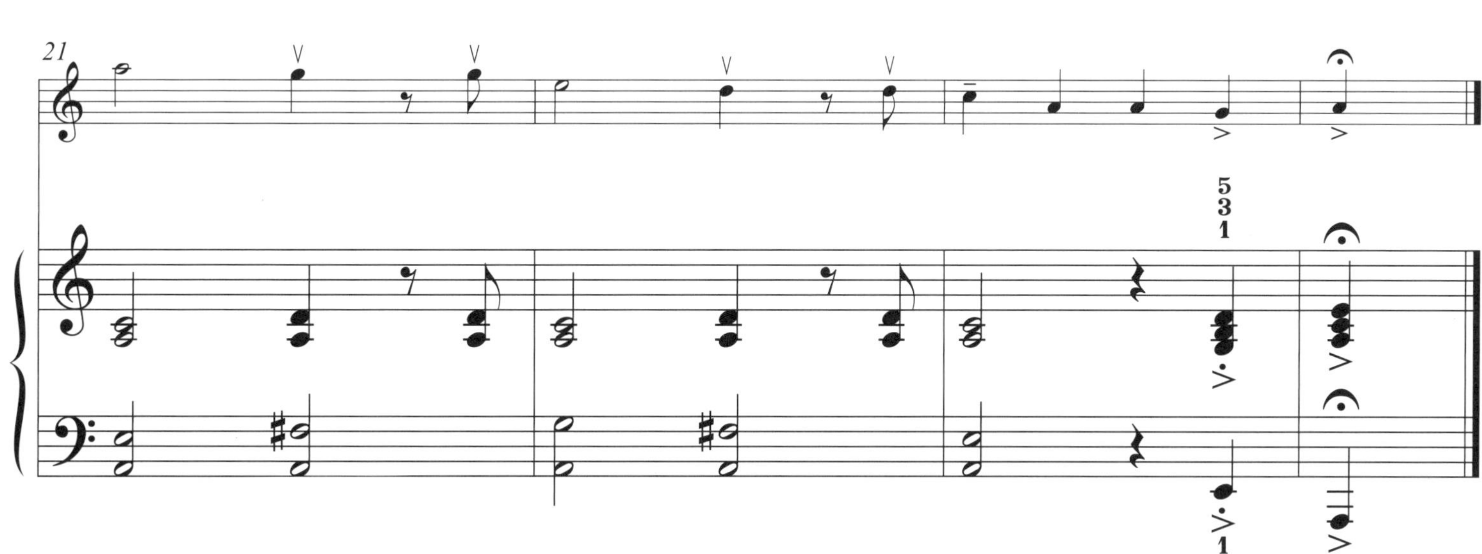
21

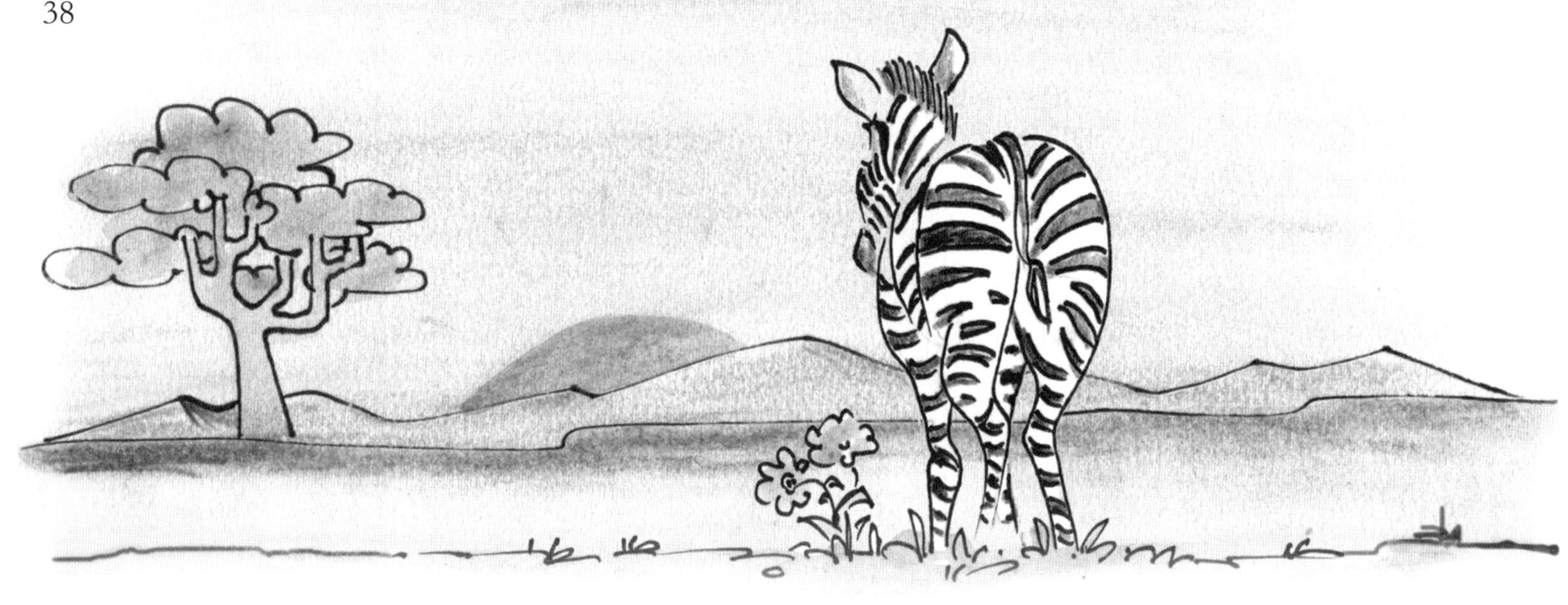

Sonnenuntergang

Sunset

Entspannt
Calmly

Karin Groß

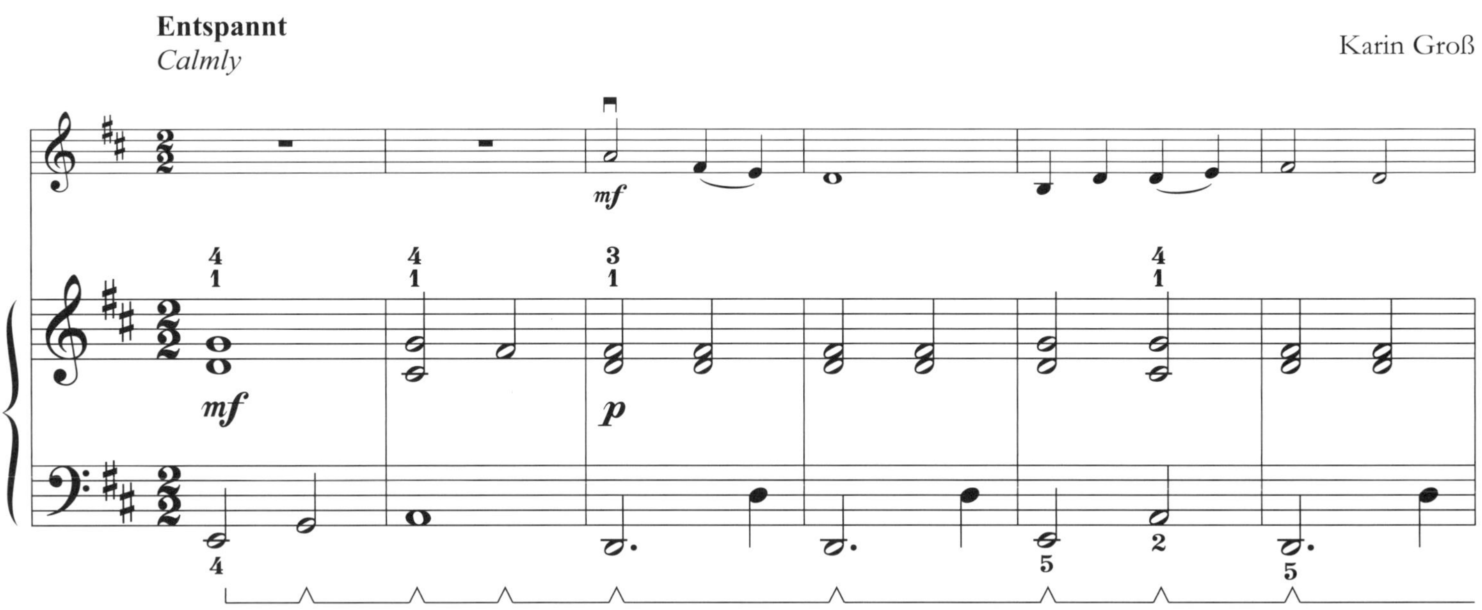

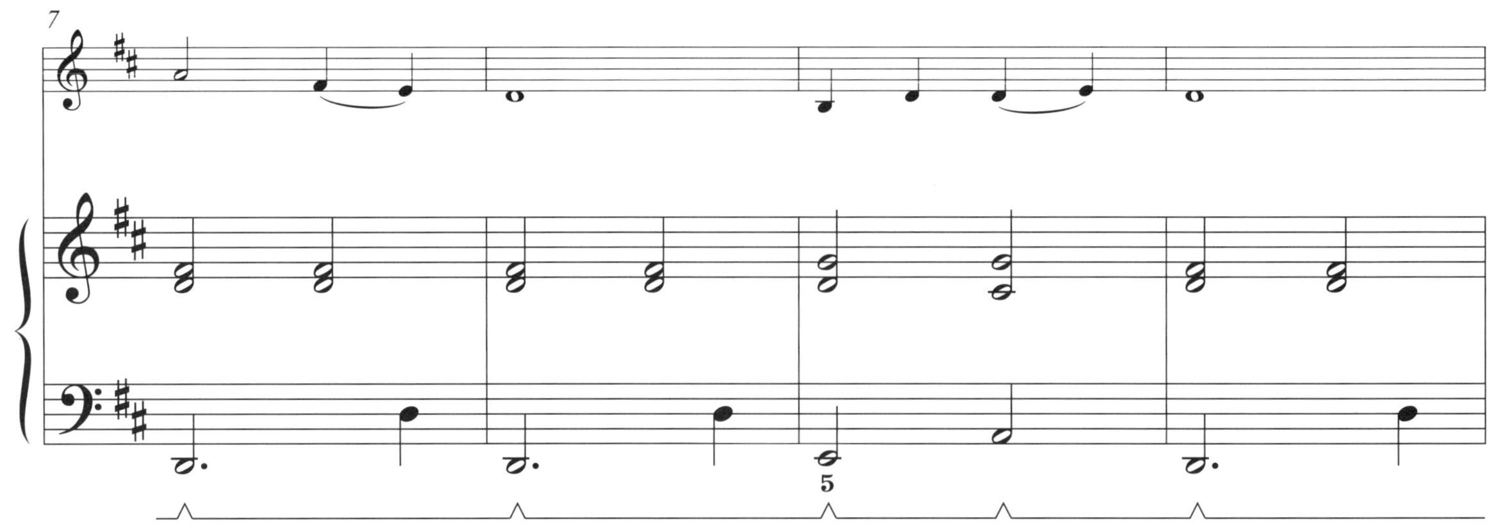

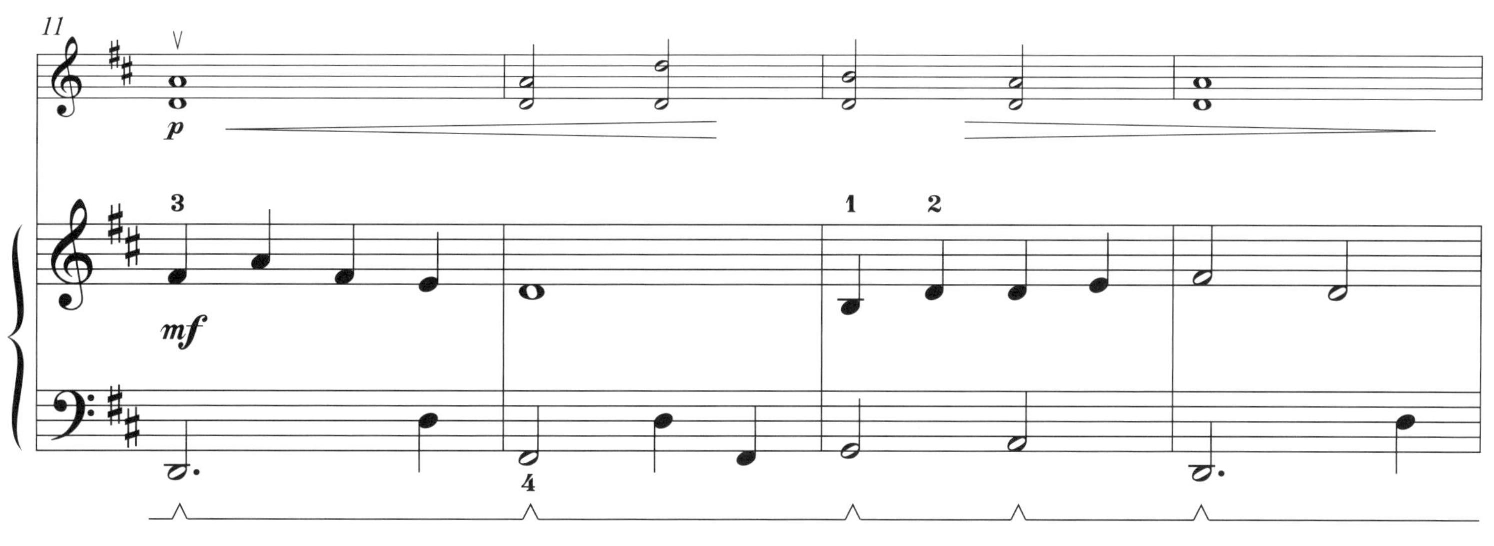
11
p
3
mf
1
2
4

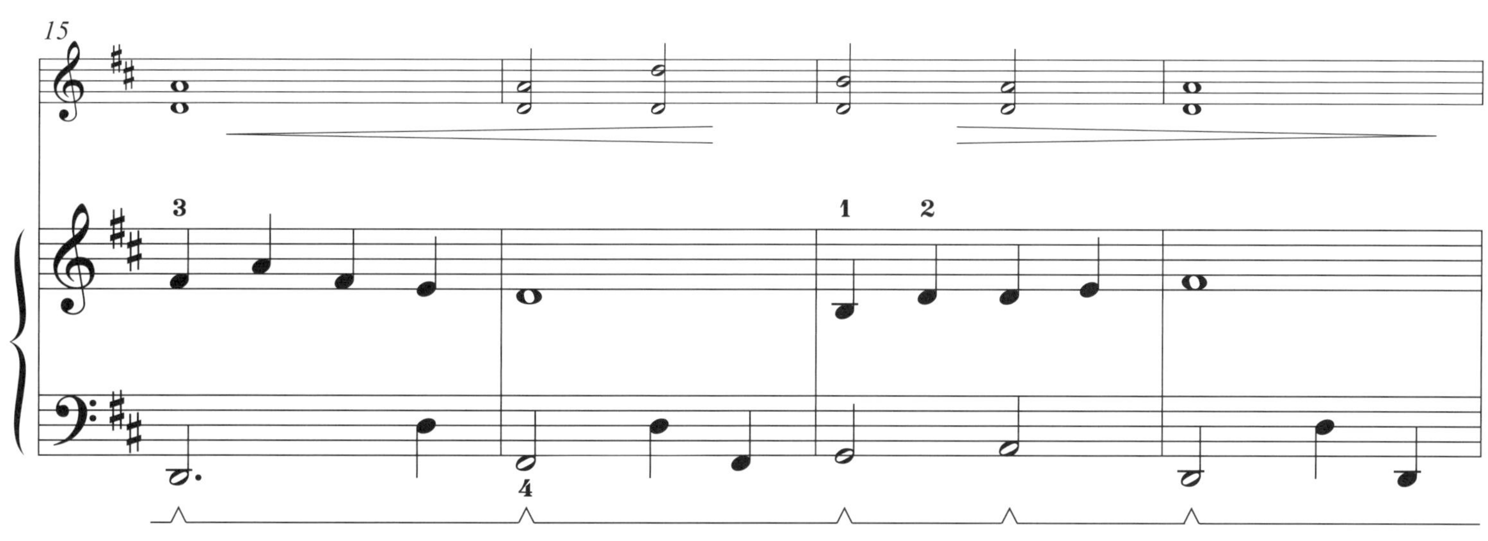
15
3
1
2
4

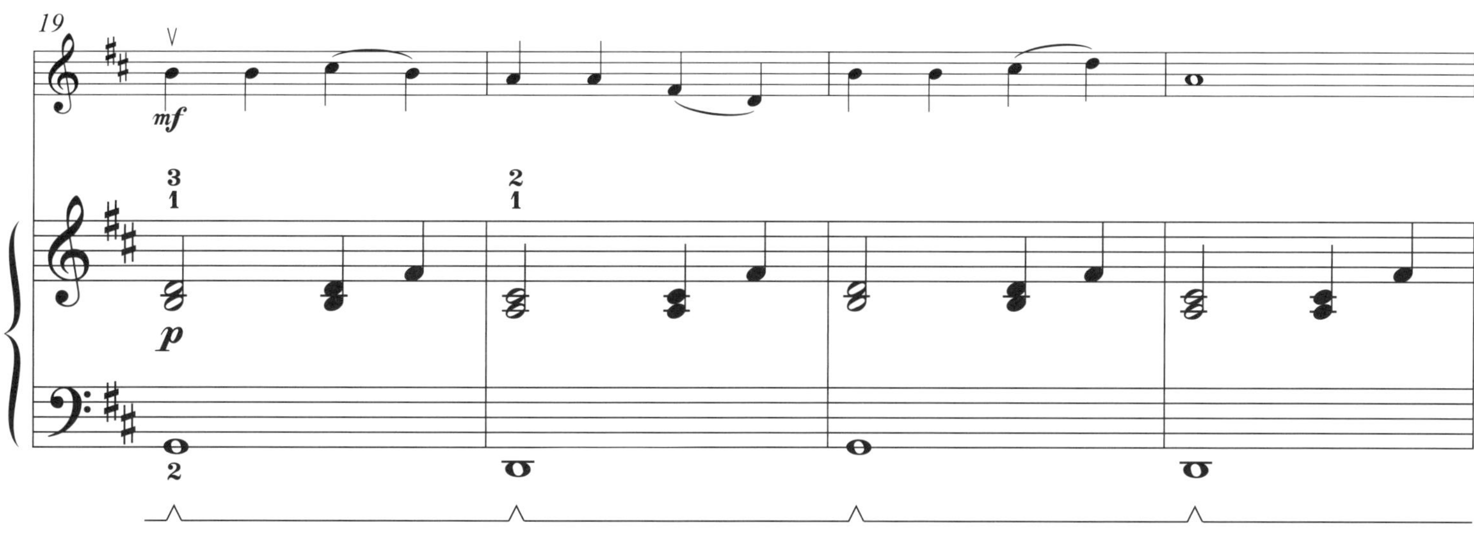
19
mf
3
1
2
1
p
2

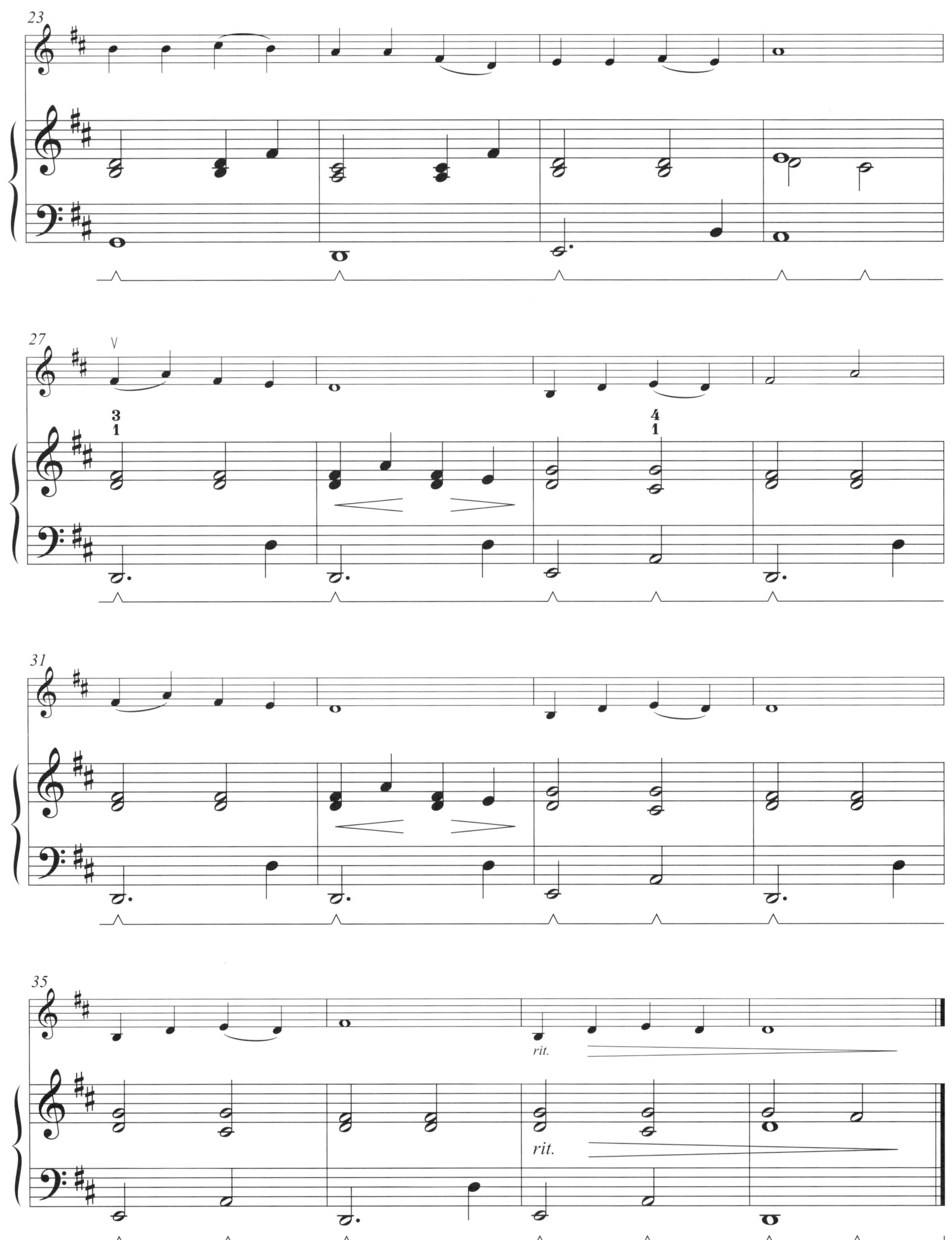
23
27
3
1
4
1
31
35
rit.
rit.

Die Joggingrunde

Let's Go Jogging

Recht schnell
Fairly quickly

Karin Groß

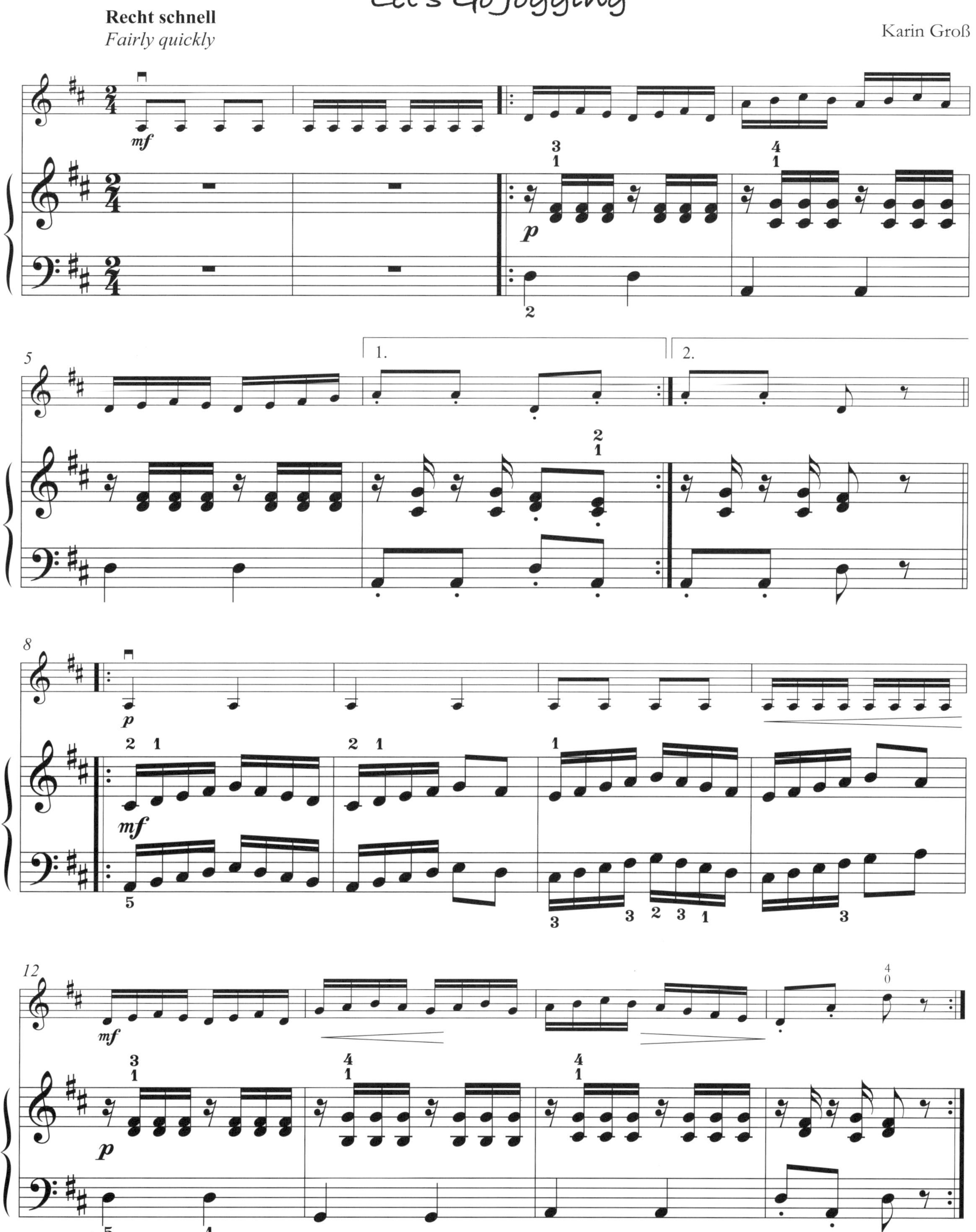

Walking Bass

Zügig ♫ = ♩ ♪ (triplet)
Briskly

Karin Groß

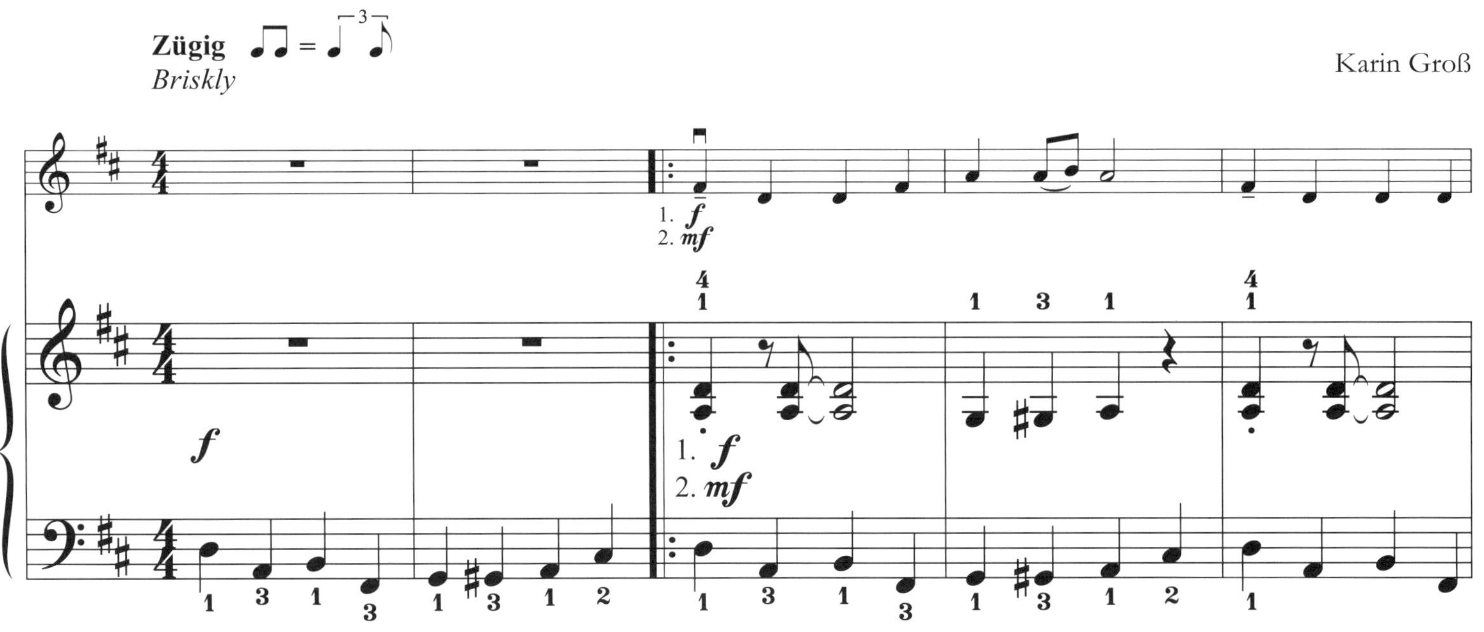

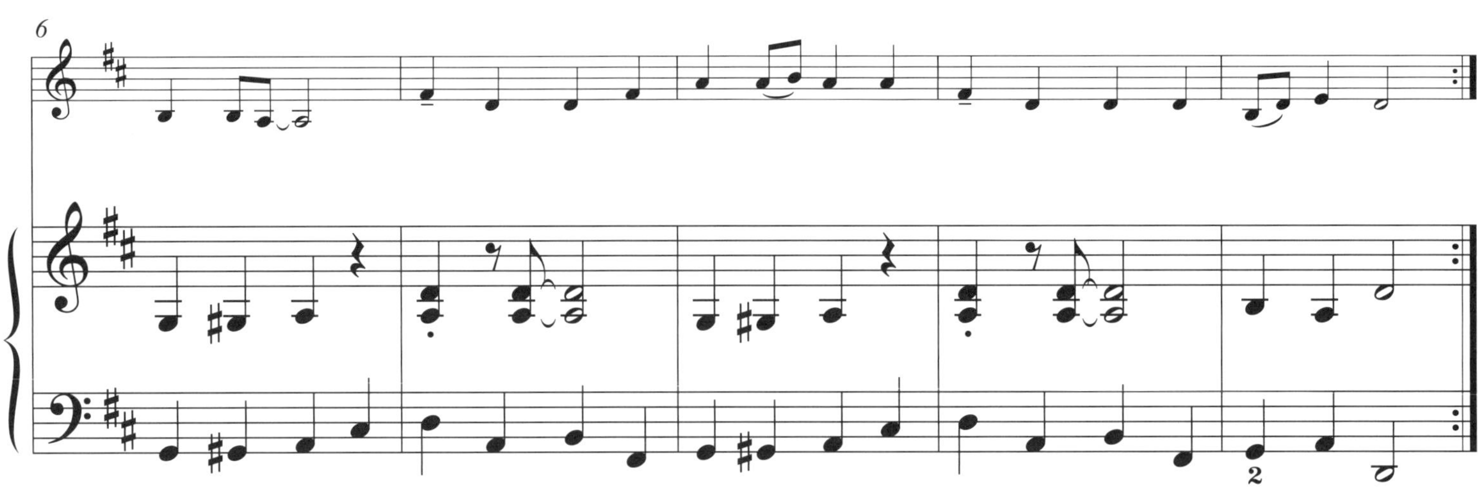

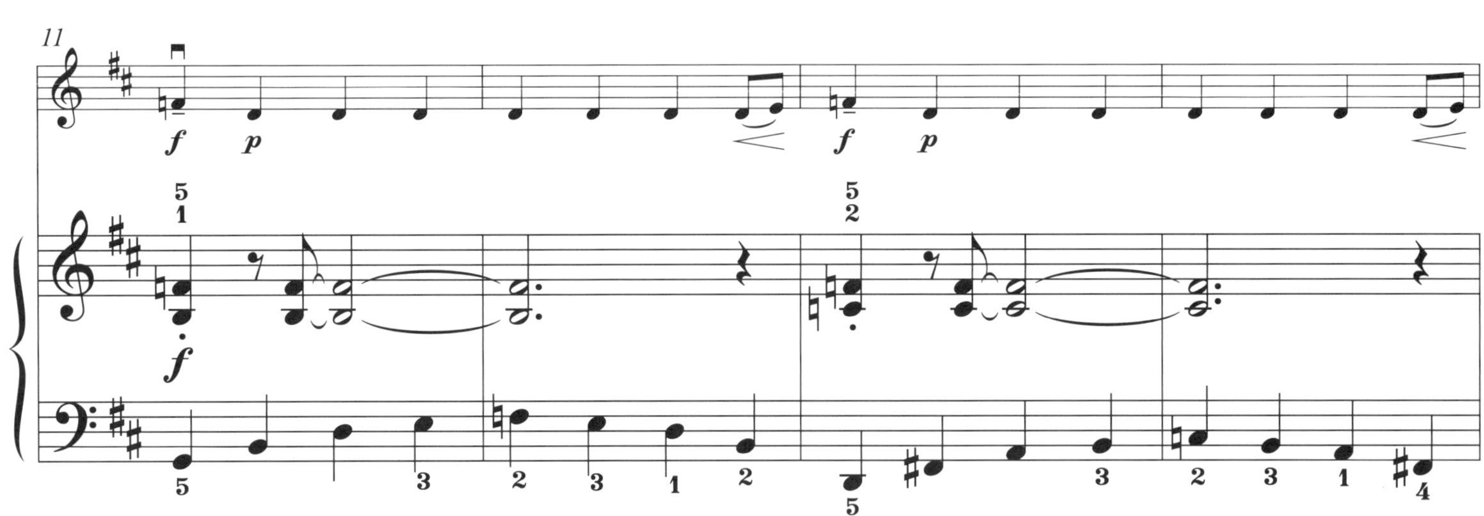

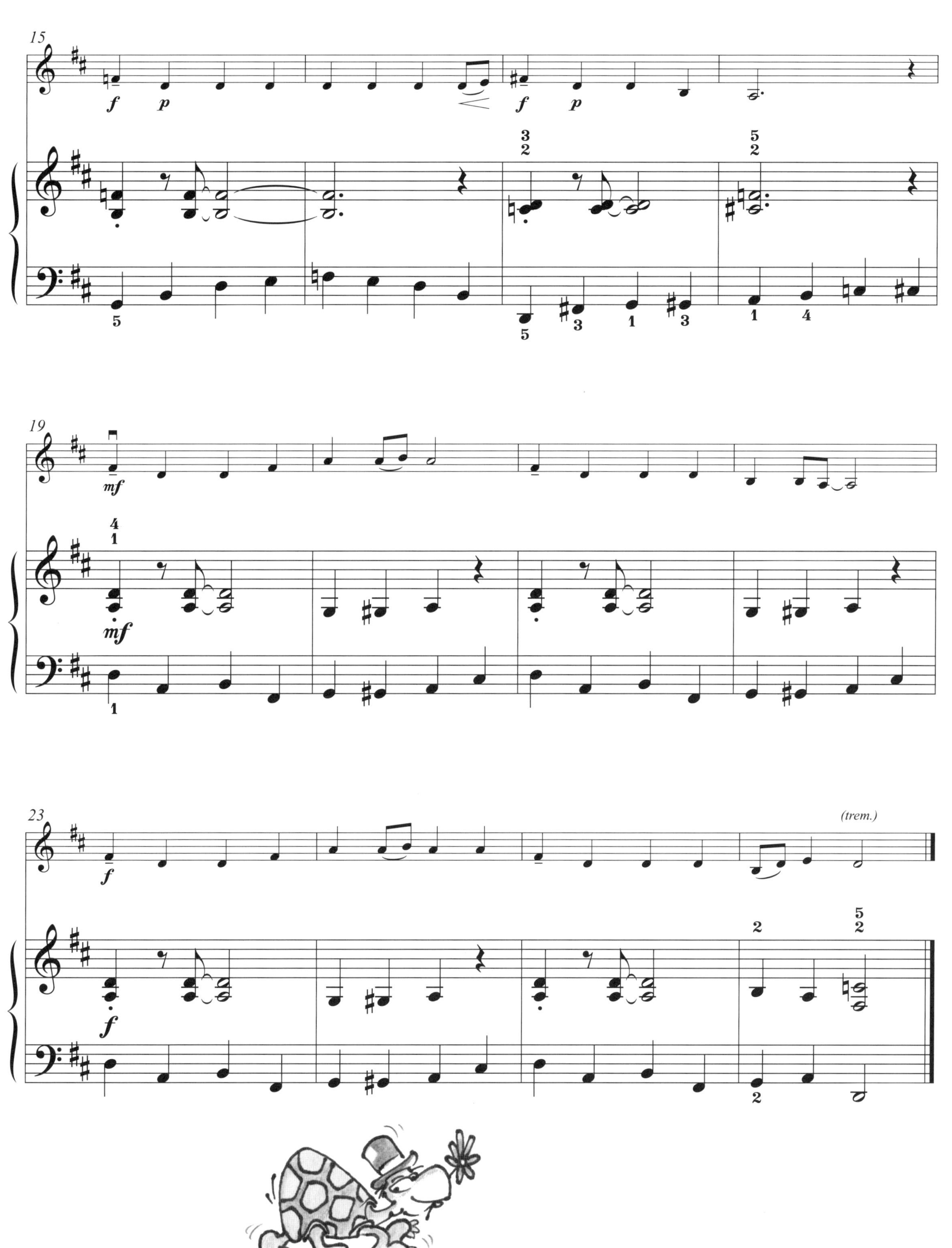
(trem.)

Es regnet in Strömen

It's Pouring Down

Fließend
Flowingly

Karin Groß

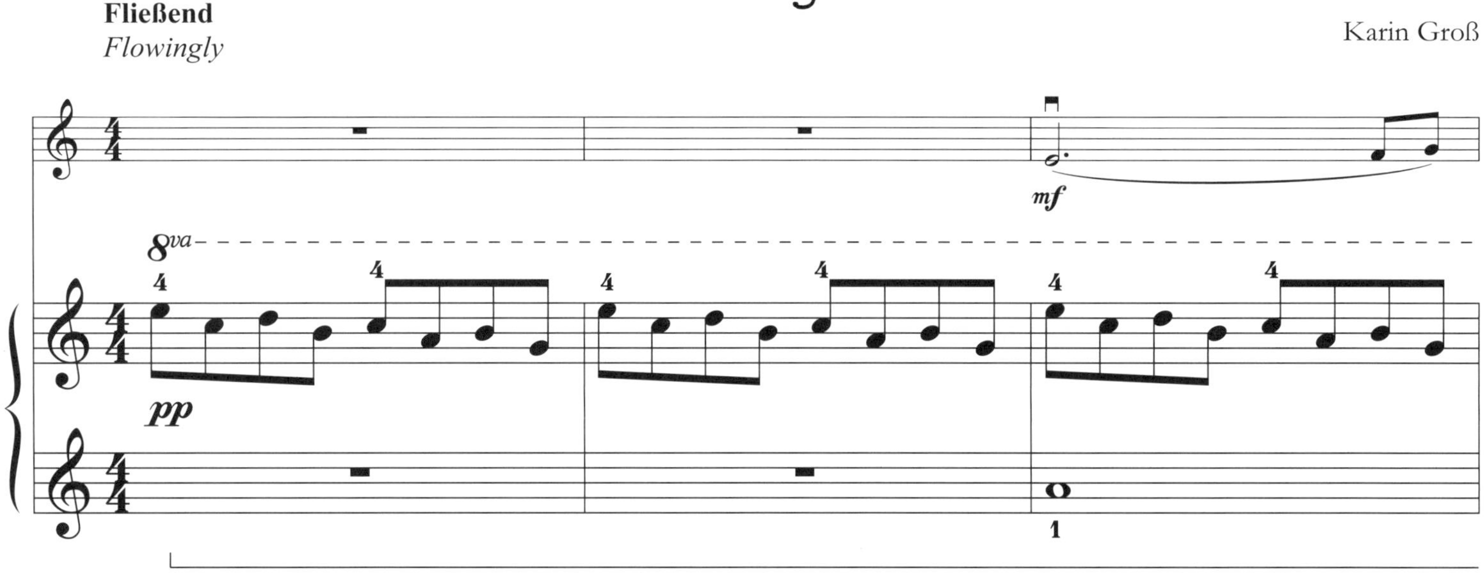

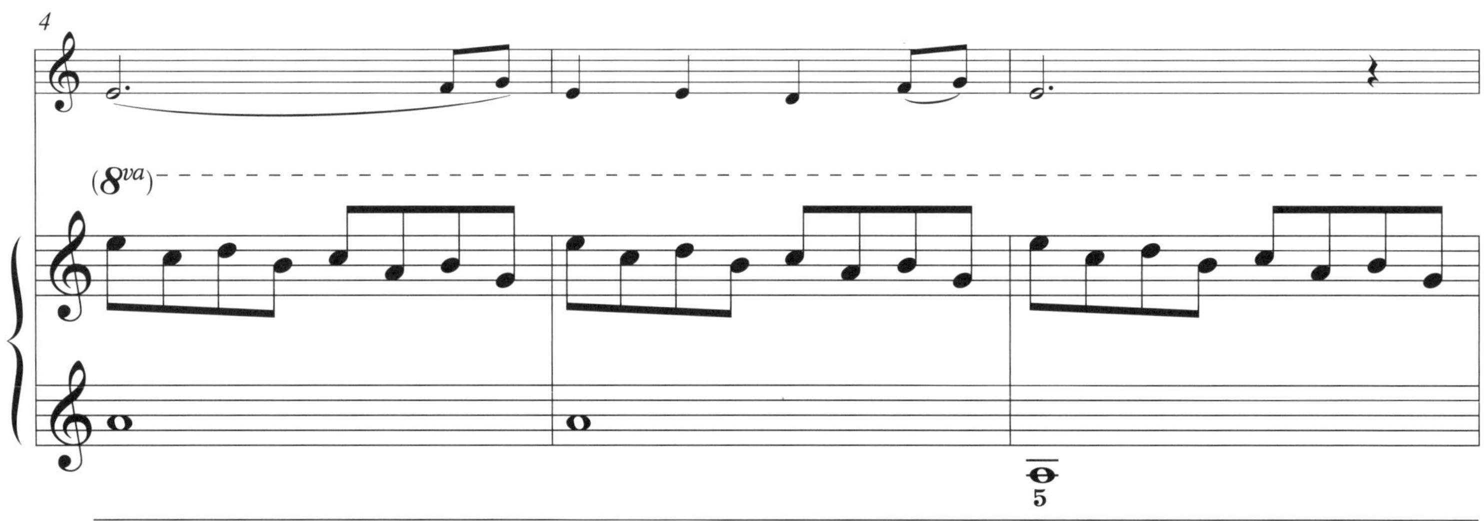

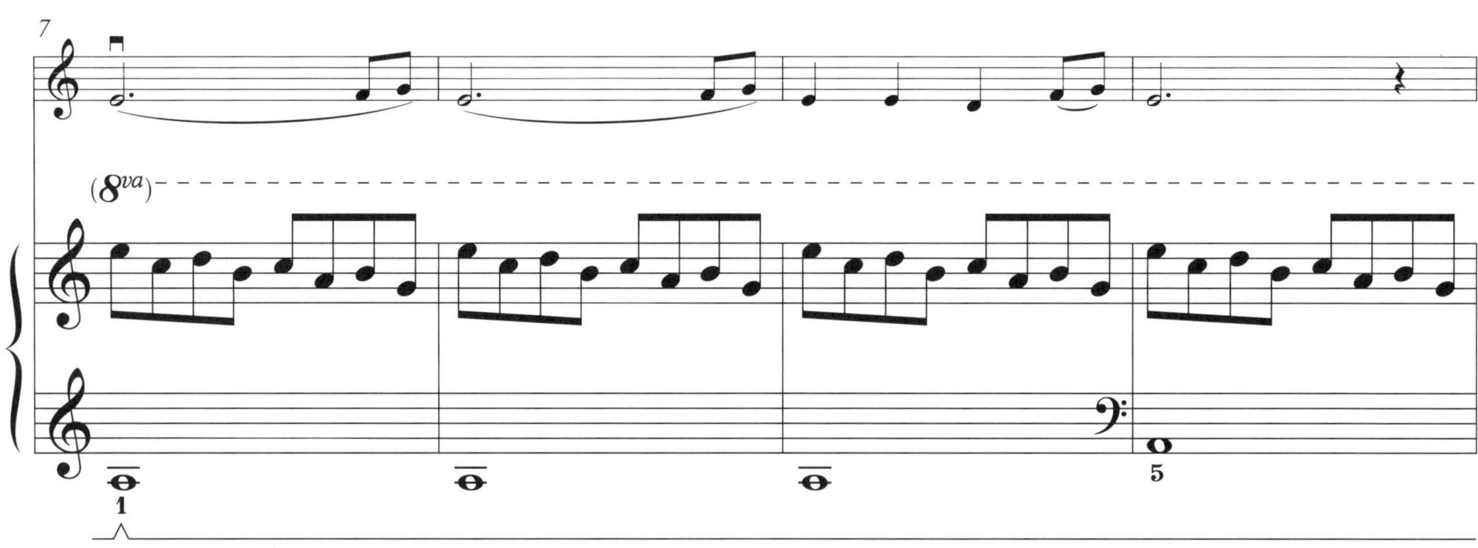

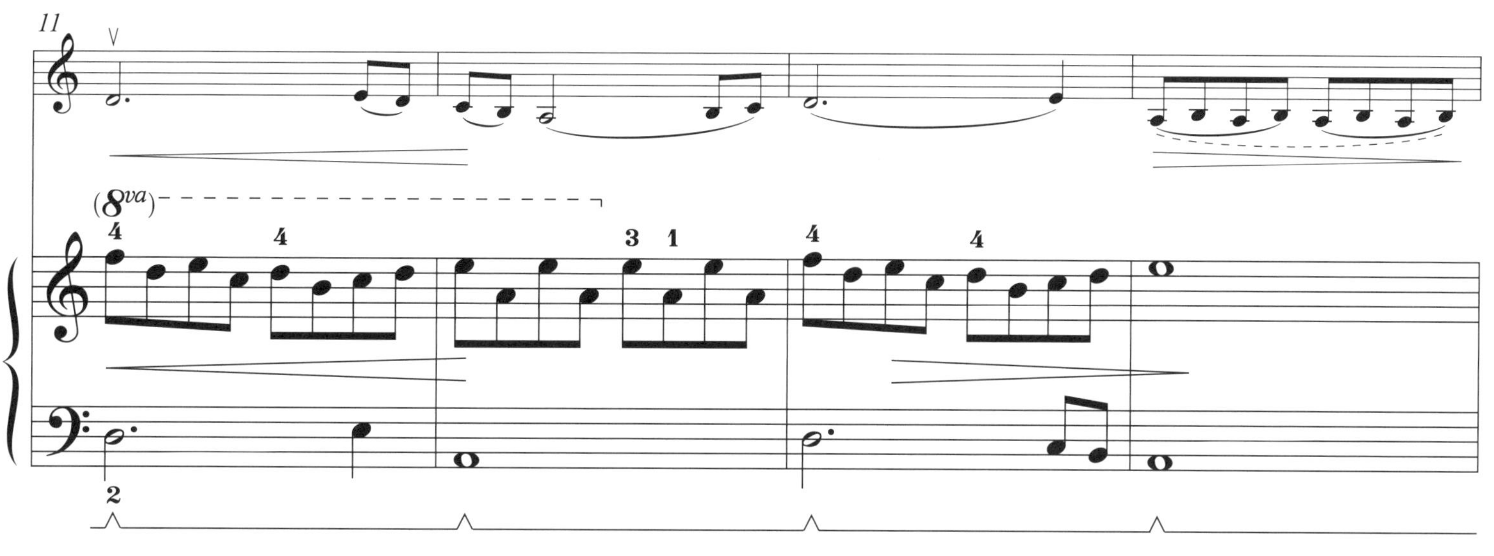
(8va)

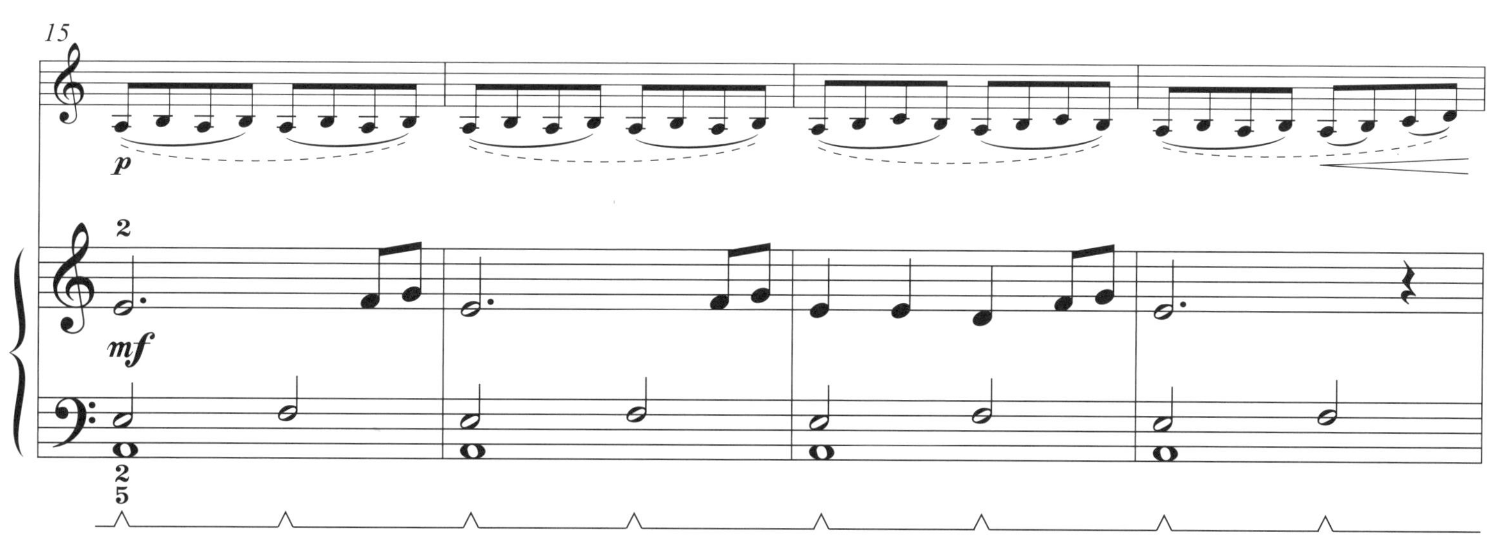
p
mf

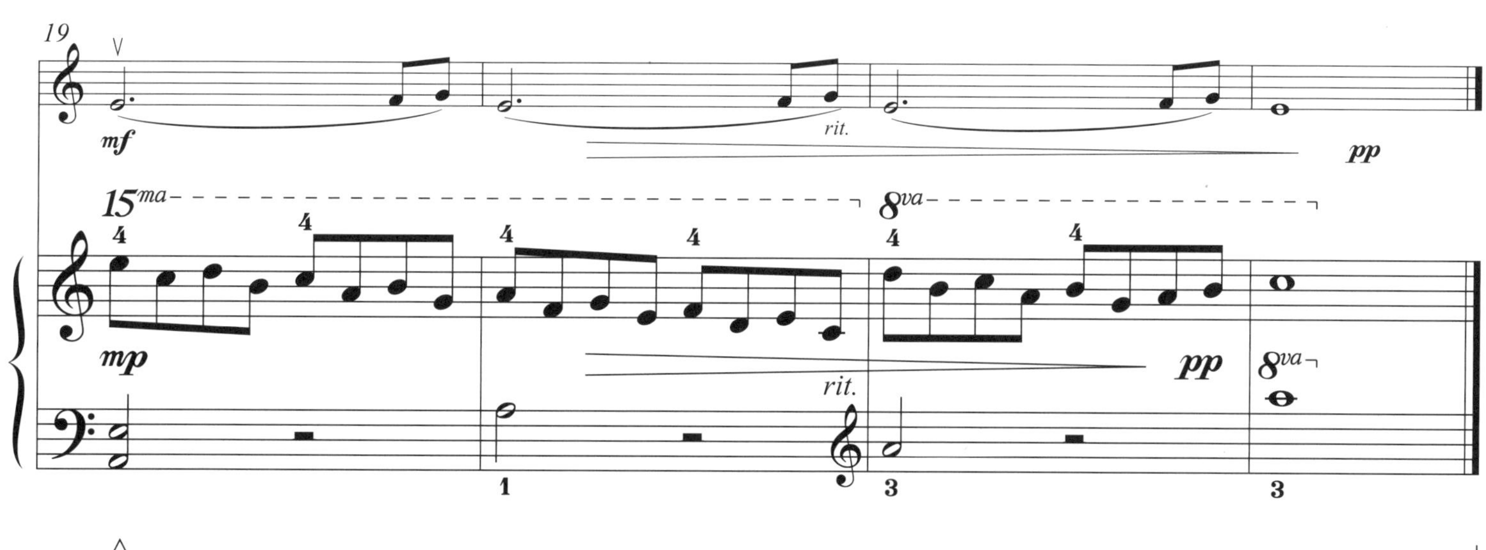
mf
rit.
pp
15ma
8va
mp
pp
rit.
8va

Auf der Ritterburg

In The Knight's Castle

Karin Groß

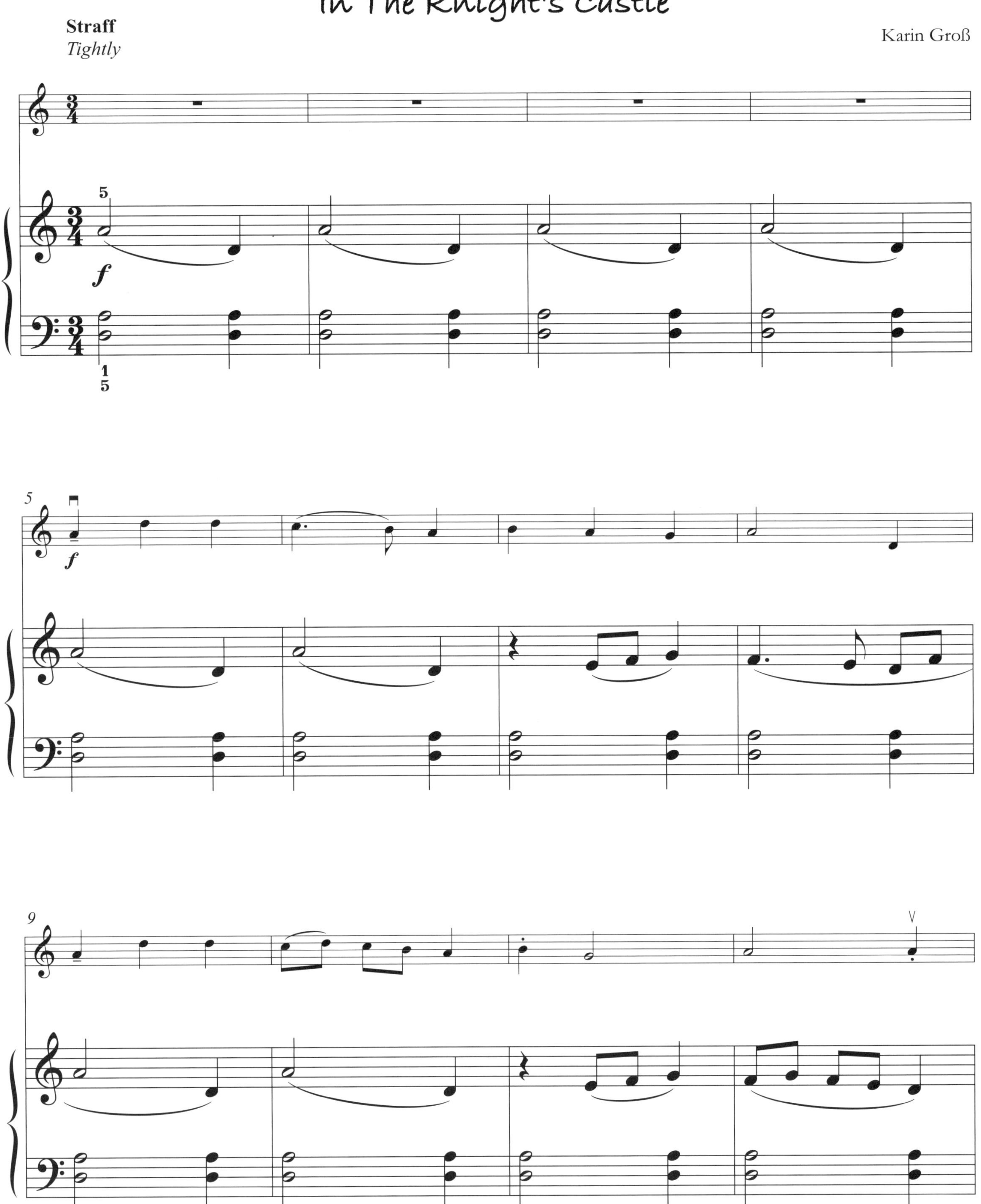

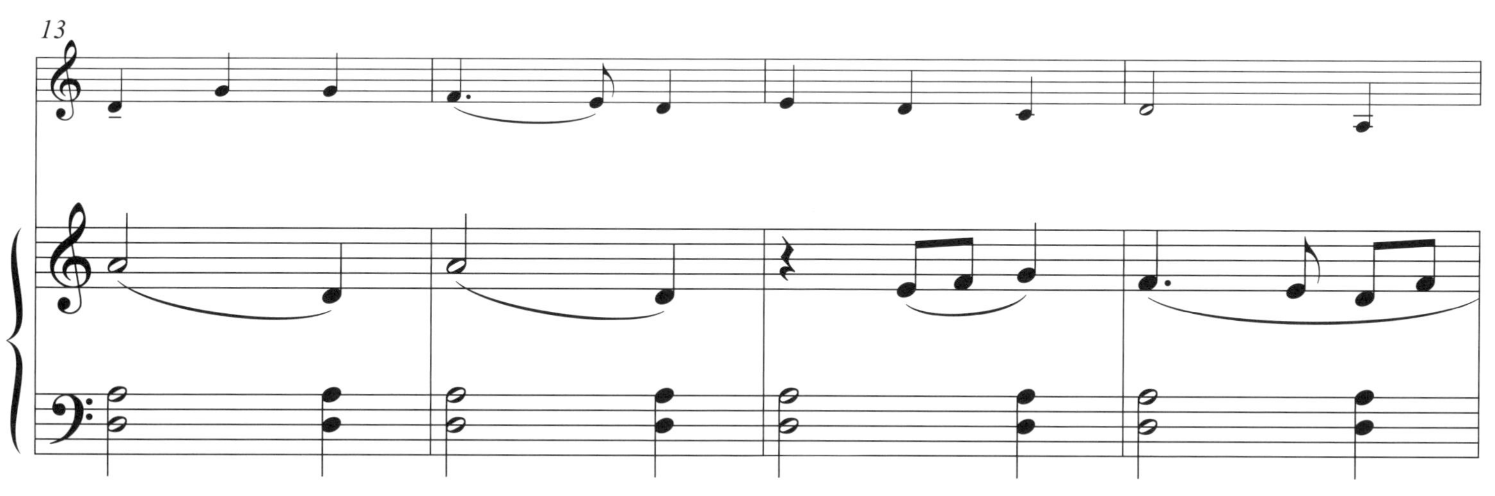
13

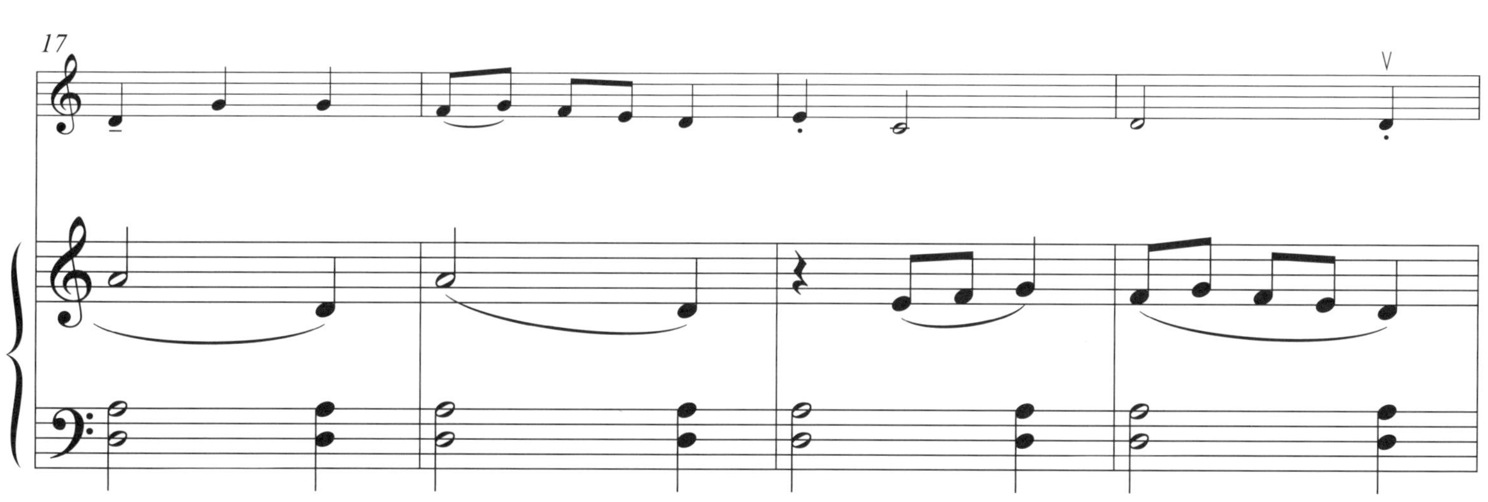
17

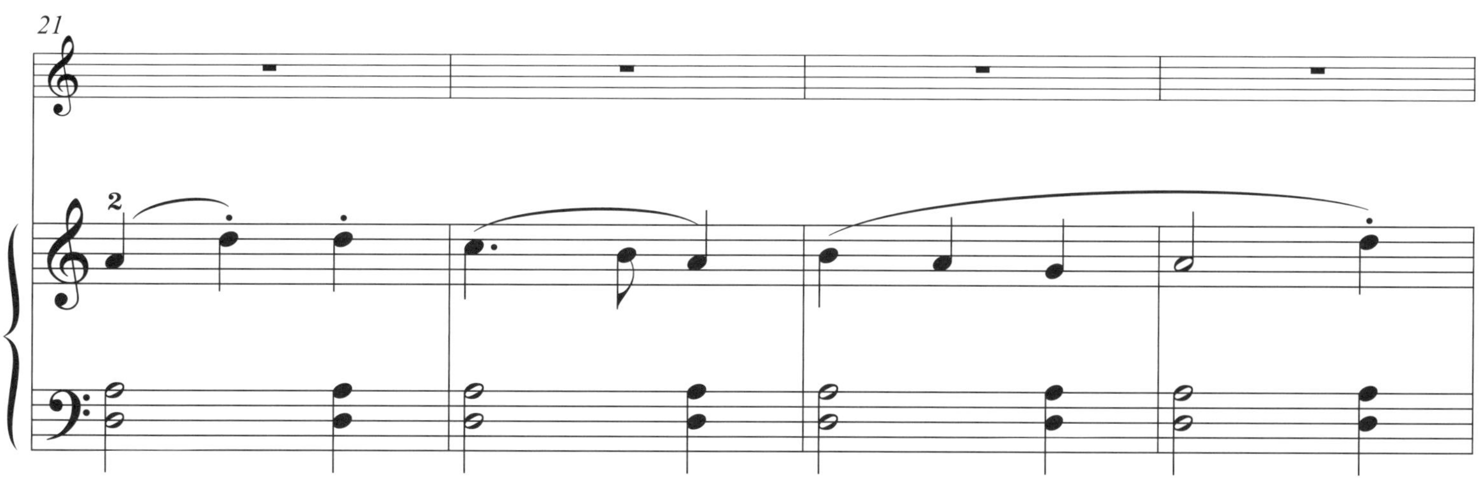
21
2

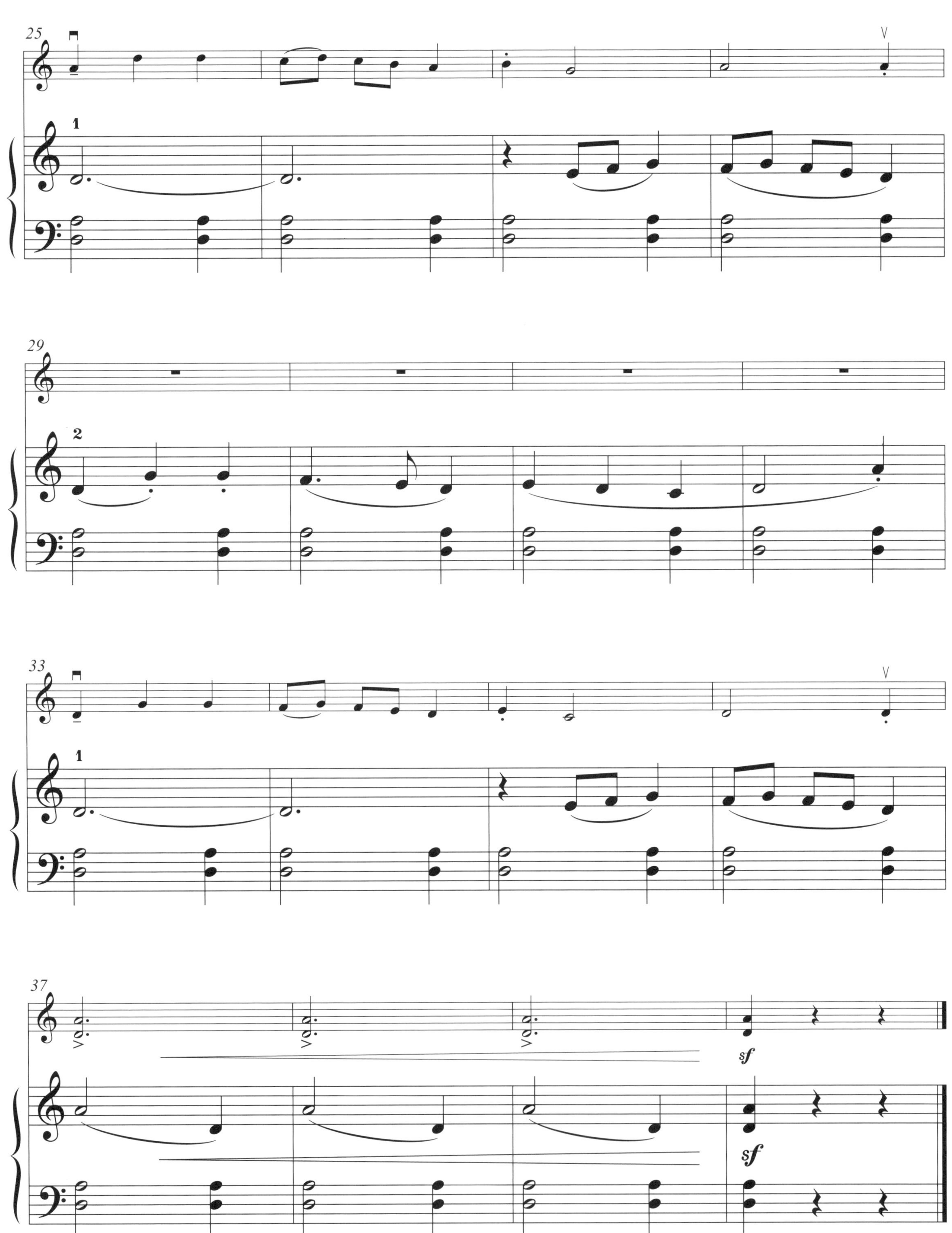
25
1
29
2
33
1
37
sf
sf